21 TOMORROWS:
HR Systems
in the Emerging Workplace
of the 21st Century

EDITED BY ROBERT H. STAMBAUGH

International
Association for
Human Resource
Information Management

21 Tomorrows: HR Systems in the Emerging Workplace of the 21st Century

An IHRIM Book
Published by Rector Duncan & Associates, Inc.
314 Highland Mall Boulevard
Austin, Texas 78752 USA

ISBN 0-9679239-0-5   US $49/$52 CAN
© 2000 by the International Association
for Human Resource Information Management
401 N. Michigan Avenue
Chicago, IL 60611 USA
All Rights Reserved
Printed in the United States of America
March 2000

Dedication

In memory of Ed Goldmacher, who contributed as much as anyone to helping IHRIM and our profession make it to the 21st century, and who would have been among the first to see our potential for going even farther now that we are here.

Table of Contents

Preface

Early last November, while I was sitting on the beach reading one of many information technology prognostications about how the world would look a decade from now, I decided to marry the concept of "just in time" publication with the power of the IHRIM network and solicit a similar series of projections about our own business. I obtained a list of Summit Award winners, past Association presidents, and industry thought leaders — and I e-mailed or called each of them and issued a simple invitation: write a 1000-2500 word article about some aspect of our business in the decade to come. Altogether, I contacted about 45 people. About two-thirds indicated an interest. Despite the competing pressures of year-end closes and the other special holiday treats that Human Resource Systems stakeholders have come to know so well over the years, over 20 articles arrived in my mail in time for inclusion in this publication. That's commitment!

Simultaneously, I asked the IHRIM Board for the funding necessary to publish and distribute this book. With only minor discussion, I obtained their seal of approval, a green light to proceed, more funding than I originally asked for, and a promise of administrative support wherever it was needed. Along the way, I even obtained commitments for an article or two! With this kind of backing from the Board, we are able to enter the new millennium with a new product already in hand — and the promise of many more to come in the following months.

As you scan the articles I've included here, you'll see that there were no predefined categories or quotas involved with the project. I assumed (rightly, as the results will show), that contributors would choose to write about a wide range of issues. I also figured — and time will tell if I was as lucky with this assumption as with the first — that the distribution of topics would be representative of the diversity and ferment in our industry as the old decade and century end. Doubtless, there are many topics that aren't addressed in this collection. There are others that received arguably too much attention. But, that's the way the project evolved. It reflects our dynamic workplace, and neither my biases nor the designs or preferences of IHRIM or its Board of Directors.

How should you use this collection? Certainly not as an HR systems map or answer book, because it raises as many questions as it answers! But here's a hint: our authors are unanimous in the opinion that things are changing at a pace that defies "dead on" predictions, and in so many directions at once that you're bound to be surprised by what confronts HRIS systems and professionals in the next few years. I'd recommend instead that you use it in some of these ways:

Weekend reading — We have purposely kept the selections here as non-technical and jargon-free as possible, so the entire volume should be easy to read and enjoy, perhaps at a single sitting. If you have time for nothing else, scan the contents, and you'll learn a great deal about the viewpoints of package vendors and consulting firms, practitioners in large and small companies, academics and interested by-standers.

Springboard for discussion — Do the ideas expressed by our expert authors sound feasible? Do they offer threat or promise for your system, or for the industry at large? Should they be forwarded to other people in your organization? Do they call into question assumptions or plans you've already made? I suggest you and a handful of peers pick one or two articles and make them the centerpiece(s) of an afternoon offsite or a department lunch discussion.

Source of scenarios — Take a handful of these articles and pretend the projections in them are accurate and have already come true. Then play back "a day in the life" of your system and ask yourselves what kind of changes would be needed if the authors included here are as prescient as we hope. Make sure your scenarios cover not only next week's possibilities, but also those at the two or three year in the future levels as well.

Senior management update — Take the results of your scenarios and make a list of what HRIS needs to function as a business partner in the future. Forward the list, along with a copy of this book to your HR Vice President and/or CIO/CKO. At worst, it will signal for them that the previously backroom function of HR systems management can and does look to the future when it plans for "technical" change. At best, it will open a dialogue between higher-level decision makers and the HRIS function — a dialogue from which we all would learn.

Because, it's the learning and the discussion that matter: if we don't take the lead in these areas, we'll be left behind by advances in other parts of human resources and information technology, and we will never catch up.

Bob Stambaugh
Kekaha, HI
March 2000

Acknowledgements

In view of the tight production schedule we adopted to assure delivery of the book while the New Year was still green, most of the authors involved put their manuscripts in my hands for editing, proofing and sense-making. I thank them all for their cooperation, commitment, and, most of all, their confidence. Where ideas come through "loud and clear," you can be sure it's their handiwork, intact and accurate. Where there's confusion or fuzziness, you can be equally sure the misunderstandings are mine alone.

I would also like to thank IHRIM and its Board of Directors for funding this effort and for providing its support throughout the process. Our "HQ" operation, Smith, Bucklin & Associates, should be thanked as well for their support and coordination. Finally, special thanks goes to Tom Faulkner of Rector Duncan & Associates for exercising his usual magic and pulling it all together in a timely manner, with no apparent effort at all.

As you can see from the cast of characters involved in this effort, it has been an IHRIM team production from the start. What we can accomplish once, we can do over and over again. I hope we will see other such publications in the near future.

Foreword

By Michael R. Losey

Yes, One More
Y2K Article!

When Bob Stambaugh asked me to write an article for this publication, I jumped at the chance, as I have a fond respect for IHRIM. SHRM and IHRIM are both longstanding members of the Council of Human Resource Management Associations (COHRMA). COHRMA is an informal group comprised of HR organizations such as SHRM, IHRIM, ASTD, ACA, HRPS, NESRA, NACE and others that share an interest in the human resource profession. We meet regularly to network and share ideas for mutual improvement.

And for this special publication, what special insight might I have? Yes, I could write about the HR profession and its related professions. I could write about the changing workplace, globalization, legislative impact on the workplace, diversity and so many other topical issues.

What I never imagined myself writing about was the predicted Y2K computer bug, since I have felt for a long time that if I saw one more article on this subject, I would be ill. But then, as I worried about Bob's December submission deadline, and just a few weeks prior to the millennium, a special TV movie highlighting all the possible pending disasters was viewed by millions. I have had it. I must write and offer another perspective.

And, of course, this article will not be seen until the year 2000. I wonder if the way I see it will be what happens.

■ A Matter of a Half Full Glass?

On a recent flight, I sat next to a gentleman who told me a story that I thought was a good Y2K parallel. This man's father passed away in 1993 and, at that time, the family invested in a headstone upon which they added the surviving mother's name. With greater permanency than any programmer's keystroke, the stone cutter carved 1932 - 19__ . I wondered why neither the family nor the stone cutter anticipated that a woman born in 1932 and alive in 1993, might live until the year 2000. For the same reason, I suspect, early programmers never considered the systems they were defining would last until the year 2000.

As an HR vice president at Unisys in 1990, I retired Dr. J. Presper Eckert who, along with Dr. John Mauchly, invented the ENIAC, generally accepted as the first working computer. But, even they could not accurately anticipate the potential of a computerized world. For instance, I once asked Dr. Eckert how many additional computers they thought they would produce after they invented the first one? His answer was "two or three." So why are we surprised when brilliant people like Eckert or those who developed the original COBOL programming language, would miss the programming consequences of dropping the first two digits of the century?

And yes, the world has been delinquent in recognizing and dealing with this issue. Seems proof again that when we do not have the time and money to do something right the first time, we always have the time, and even more money, to fix it later?

■ But what is the bright side of this Y2K issue?

First of all, fixing the Y2K problem — at a cost of billions — has happened during a rosy U.S. economy and a period of good business profits. Think of it, all of the recent high profits and Federal budget surpluses have been net of these significant Y2K costs. What a disaster it would have been to absorb these costs during a recession with lower or non-existent profits.

Secondly, despite the fact that we have spent a great deal of money fixing this problem, it is an investment. Many companies have addressed the Y2K issue by upgrading or purchasing entirely new systems. Notwithstanding the possible short-term disruption, there will be the long-term benefit of more powerful, advanced systems. This may be the ultimate prize, especially for the United States given its historical leadership in information systems development and utilization.

Yes, just after the stroke of midnight on December 31st, surely there will be some problems. All of us have experienced attempts to replace an existing software program with new shrink wrapped, off the shelf, software. Too often, we witness how even these well-tested and mass produced products can have unexpected problems or interfere with other programs.

As I write this article, most of the work required for our businesses, organizations and governments to be Y2K compliant is supposed to be done. By the time people read this article, we will know.

But, I also predict that unlike election results, Hawaii and the West Coast will not just be watching the East Coast to see what happens. We will watch Guam and the other Marshall Islands — where the sun first rises on U.S. soil each day. We will then follow the sun and clock as it travels to the West including many underdeveloped countries where more may go wrong than in more developed countries. Then, we will watch Africa and Europe and wait for the wave to finally hit the eastern mainland.

Yes, January 1, 2000 will be a long and closely watched day. But, eventually we shall all benefit from this feared Y2K millennium crisis. Tools effectively used by humans have contributed greatly to the advancement of civilization. However, never in the history of the world has any tool been updated as of a required date to meet a common, higher level of performance. The Y2K legacy will be how it positioned us for higher levels of productivity and better lives.

Michael R. Losey is the President, Society for Human Resource Management, North American Human Resource Management Association, and the World Federation of Personnel Management Associations. He can be reached at **mlosey@shrm.org**.

Introduction

By Robert H. Stambaugh

This diverse set of essays about the future of human resources and HRIS offers an insight or two into almost every aspect of the business as we know it today — and as it is likely to evolve in the decade to come. In just about every area, our authors predict constant, unrelenting change — and it's a kind of change with which few of us are familiar: erratic, non-linear, complex and interconnected, always somewhere in the background or around the corner. If there's a single message that can be distilled from the collection as a whole, it's something about the wild ride we're just beginning.

What kind of systems will we be using — ERP? ERP "light"? Some variation of today's client/server systems? Or will they be something else — something we haven't seen or thought of in late 1999. Who will own the systems we'll be using — HR? The overall "enterprise" within which HR operates? Could IT be the owner of record? Those are just the internal options. What about an outside agency where our outsourced programs run?

And, then there are the really tough questions. Who will be the system stakeholders? Lynne Mealy and Row Henson each offer a view of the workplace and the demographics that act as a backdrop to this question. And their answers, while different in the details, both point out the need to rethink and offer modes of interaction and analytic/interpretive capabilities that will appeal to the different generations of stakeholders who will be sharing the workplace of the next decade or so.

Who will help us make sense of the software and its uses in this world, with its dizzying social and organizational change? Karen Beaman sees the answer to this question as a challenge for the consulting firms we know now, as well as some others we'll likely see in the future. But, the nature of consulting and consultants will have changed as well, contributing yet another uncertainty factor to our mix.

But, will the systems that we hope are "just over the horizon" really solve the problems HRIS has been promising to address for the last quarter century? Sid

> *Regardless of where*
>
> *your company is situated*
>
> *along the continuum . . .*
>
> *it's time to get moving.*

Simon, an IHRIM co-founder, draws upon his experience as vendor, consultant and practitioner, and gives us a resounding "NO." As a "north of the border" observer who can address this issue with perhaps a little more detachment than most of us, Al Doran isn't any more sanguine. In fact, he points out several paradoxes in the way vendors build, sell and market their products and services. If our experts are right, we shouldn't look to the vendor world for the answers to our problems.

Do we blame the vendors for too much "hype" and overselling of their wares? Before you answer, read the contributions from Mike Smith (voice response, call centers, and where that aspect of the business is going in the future) and Ren Nardoni (succession planning in an increasingly complex and uncertain world). You'll see thoughtful and reasoned plans for upgrades and enhancements, so it's hard to lay the full blame for failure to deliver at the vendors' feet.

Indeed, a voice from higher education, Miriam Ward, addresses self-service and in many ways, validates where the vendors want to go! Rick Olivieri, a Silicon Valley compensation and systems expert, offers a similar treatment of the compensation function.

Part of the reason for the perception of non-delivery and non-responsiveness has to stem from the sheer diversity of the population our vendors are trying to serve. Read Paul Piper's view of the future — and his surprise prediction about the future of HR — and then immediately compare it to Ruth Ladner's view. You'll see two HR worlds, both likely to exist before the decade is over.

And, we will need plans for supporting all of them. Plans require some sort of structure — a stable framework around which we can hang the diverse and evolving parts of our own businesses. In view of the complex and varied challenges we'll be addressing, it's highly unlikely we will all be comfortable with the same framework and structure. Part of the reason for our uneasiness with the "one plan" approach is the sheer diversity of systems "out there." No one structure will be right for everyone. Dr. John Sullivan offers an academic/consultant way of looking at the overall HRIS field and where it appears to be headed — for different reasons, at different speeds, in different industries. Joel Lapointe offers a complementary view of the industry, from a large consultancy perspective. As a balance, we have a similar characterization of the market and the challenge from Jim Spoor — an HRIS package vendor and service provider.

So, what do we do in this world of change? Some corporate strategies and their accompanying HR/HRIS support agendas will choose a cautious, slow, incremental path for change. Others will jump in with both feet now. Regardless of where your company is situated along the continuum between those two extremes, it's time to get moving. Our contributors offer some help here as well.

From his consultant's perspective, Marc Miller offers an action plan for executives that you might consider as a baseline agenda for HR managers in the decade to come. Rest assured, some variation of what he recommends will be in play every year, from now until decades end. Likewise, Mike Method details some of the same issues and responses from a practitioner's standpoint. You'll probably come up with an approach that borrows from both of them. Add Dave Russo's view — a rare mix of HR and HRIS management background — and you'll appreciate the need to go beyond making the system work, to delivering results that can be used in the workplace. Altogether, this trio paints a challenging mural for our future.

You'll also need to involve IT more closely than you have ever done — or wanted to do —in the past. John Macy, weighing in from Australia and delivering one proof that our discipline's "opportunities and challenges" are truly world wide, highlights a number of more IT-oriented prescriptions for action and planning. They're the launching pad for your "technical" conversations.

Conversation? Coordination? Communication? Virtually every contributor to our collection stresses somewhere the need for and the value associated with close and constant communication and dialogue in our profession. We appear to be migrating from a profession of individual contributors to a composite of teams and communities that are learning to share a lot of experience, knowledge and risk. I point to the Internet as the "great facilitator" for this whole process, but it's really a "chicken and the egg" issue: did the Internet explode because we had finally reached the critical organization mass to demand it? Or, did we begin to change the way we organize and do business because the Net had finally arrived.

It doesn't matter. For the remainder of the decade, learning to use and leverage the Internet is our discipline's 800-pound gorilla.

Valdis Krebs sees networks — impossible without our wired world — at the center of tomorrow's business: indeed, in his view they are becoming tomorrow's business. Bob Stambaugh sees them as the common denominator in any attempt at building a framework for business as a whole in the decade to come, and then for leveraging the structure to create a knowledge-oriented HR operation. From Spain, Juan Vila's contribution also addresses wired workplaces, knowledge and the enterprise — illustrating the worldwide nature of the issues we have to face. All three contributors pose some serious questions you'll have to resolve before you can really arrive at the power of the Net.

Once you've read all the selections, you'll perhaps share one or two of my conclusions. First, I am amazed at how far we have come since the days of the first mainframe-based packages for payroll processing. I'm even more in awe of the technology we can now bring to bear on our HR problems. I'm pleasantly surprised to see that the "bits and bytes" faction of HRIS has receded into the background, at least for the moment. I'm likewise delighted to see attention finally turning from "acquisition-only" mindsets, to a broader view that acknowledges the need for making information useful to all our system stakeholders — even if we still have a way to go before we can deliver on the promise.

When you re-read this book, keep that lesson in mind: we're part of a living and growing system and network of systems.

But, it's one overarching conclusion I hope you'll also share. Being a part of a field where so many questions remain unanswered and where so much remains to be done isn't all that bad: if we didn't have frustration, unmet needs and dissatisfied stakeholders, it would be a certain signal that we (and our systems) have become marginal. When you re-read this book, keep that lesson in mind: we're part of a living and growing system and network of systems. And, as long as the growth continues, we'll be meeting challenges and writing about what's over the next HRIS horizon.

And, as Mike Losey so clearly reminds us, what's over that horizon is people.

"The future ain't what it used to be."
—Yogi Berra

By Lynne Mealy

Contemplating the future of HR management systems, I was confronted with the age-old question of which came first, the chicken or the egg. Or, in this case, the technology (management systems) or human resources. For this article, I have chosen human resources, or more specifically, the workforce and the challenges it will pose to HR over the next 10 years. Predicting how technology will allow an organization to deal effectively and successfully with the HR issues of the future is easier if you first have an understanding of the factors shaping today's workforce and that of the 2000s.

What are the key HR factors as we enter the 21st century? Choice, flexibility and agility — not only in how we structure our HR programs and policies, but also in the way we deliver those programs to employees. The value of these factors, in both our HR programs and delivery methods, is evident when you look at the American economic and corporate landscape and the composition of the workforce.

■ Economics/Labor Market

The last seven years have seen a strong growth in jobs and rise in wages. Unemployment has fallen to its lowest rate in 29 years and it is expected that low unemployment levels will continue for the next 10 years. Job growth will occur primarily in the service sector, especially among jobs that require a high level of technological skills. Current job functions will not remain static, and we will also see an increased need for a higher level of skills in these positions. According to the U.S. Department of Commerce, by 2006 nearly half of all U.S. workers will be employed in industries that produce or intensively use information technology, products and services.

One of the largest influences on the future of the workplace ...

is the group of people born in the 1960s and 1970s,

referred to as Generation X.

On the flip side, poverty has not abated and literacy remains a concern. Unemployment for the disadvantaged, while decreasing, remains too high in comparison to the total labor market. Education and training will be key to improving the skills and, thus, employability of this group.

Dollars spent on benefits grew more rapidly than those spent on wages and salaries during most of the 1980s and the first half of the 1990s. Since 1995, when benefits accounted for 28 percent of workers' compensation, the growth in benefits expenditures slowed as employers increasingly chose to offer programs such as flexible spending accounts and cafeteria-style benefits aimed at controlling expenses. The need for cost containment will continue, as population aging is likely to contribute to higher average medical care costs, further increasing the cost of employer-provided health insurance.

■ Demographics

The major force in the labor market for the past 20 years, making up about 47 percent of the workforce, is the generation born in the wake of the World War II — the Boomer Generation. The youngest baby boomers are just reaching 40 years of age and thus will continue to be a force in the workplace for many years. As the first of the baby boomers reach the age of 65 within the next 10 years and ease their way into retirement, they will influence the creation and revision of corporate retirement and pension plans.

This generation defines success by upward mobility, measuring how much they can gain, climbing the corporate ladder and financial security (think Yuppie). They also have a strong set of ideals and traditions, tend to be family oriented and socially fairly liberal (think aging hippie). U.S. baby boomers have benefited from the employment related laws and legislation enacted over the past 30 years, including the U.S. Civil Rights Acts of 1963 and 1991, the U.S. Equal Pay Act, U.S. Age Discrimination in Employment Act and the U.S. Family and Medical Leave Act. As a result, many of the current HR policies and procedures have been developed for and by this generation, and HR systems developed to ensure corporate compliance with these laws.

One of the largest influences on the future of the workplace — not by size but by changes in their work styles and expectations — is the group of people born in the 1960s and 1970s, referred to as Generation X. Generation X-ers grew up in an era that saw a rise in divorce rates and an increase in the number of single family and non-traditional households and working parents. The term "latchkey children" defined this generation, referring to a population that is fiercely independent and self-reliant. They were left with a natural aptitude for multi-tasking as they filled after school hours with band, sports and part-time work. This independence also resulted in employees who greatly value job flexibility and the freedom to adjust their work schedules to fit their lifestyles.

This same generation also grew up in the era of acquisition and mergers and subsequent corporate downsizing (witnessing the layoffs of their parents) and, thus, doesn't believe in job security. Companies can no longer use long-term security such as pension plans in exchange for loyalty. Instead, these employees are interested in developing the skills that will make them more valuable in the job market. Traditional, formal recognition and performance appraisal programs are inadequate for this group that wants to know, on a frequent basis, they are making a difference and contributing to the success of the company.

Generation Y . . .

they are

the standard bearers

of the technological revolution,

having never known

anything else.

HR policies that were developed for the Baby Boomer generation will not transfer to this workforce. To keep generation X-ers motivated you must give them sufficient training resources, latitude to define problems, and derive creation solutions with rapid feedback and rewards.

Coming up fast on the heels of the generation X-ers is Generation Y (also referred to as the Net Generation, the Nintendo Generation, and the Millennials) — today's children age 14 and younger. This is the first cyber-literate generation. They live in a world that is increasingly interactive, communications-intensive and knowledge-based. They are the standard bearers of the technological revolution, having never known anything else. In a survey by the U.S. Census Bureau, 30% of children ages 3-17 used a personal computer in some location (primarily schools) in 1984; by 1997 this level had risen to 75%.

Chat rooms and e-mail are a common mode of communication. The Internet creates for the generation Y-ers an environment for contact without face-to-face relationships, even as these relationships are very important to them. For this generation, change is constant and its members look for meaning in the moment. They process information in narrative images and, thanks to electronic media, are in need of continual "hits." The challenge for software developers will be to ensure that the products used by this generation are stimulating and capable of holding their attention. Gray on gray or applications that look like Excel worksheets will not pass muster in the future. Software developers may need to take the request for bells and whistles literally. Otherwise, the generation Y-ers will move onto the next application or build it themselves.

The emphasis on training and development is forcing companies to look at technology, especially the Internet, to deliver these programs more effectively.

■ Corporate and HR Environment

Corporate growth will be strongest in small to medium-sized companies, as they are able to react more quickly to shifts in the global economy. Large corporations will also find themselves overlooked by the generation X workforce as the entrepreneurial spirit and relaxed climate of the smaller (especially start-ups) firms appeal to them.

The 3Rs of the corporate environment will continue into the 21st century — restructuring, reorganizing and reducing (the workforce). Competitive pressures will force companies to downsize as headcount and the subsequent costs associated with an employee are being reduced via layoffs, outsourcing, and the increased use of a contingent workforce. The focus on expense control will also put pressure on organizations to capitalize on the investments they made during the 90s with client/server systems and ERPs.

Even with further staff reductions, there will be an increase in the number of highly skilled jobs. Thus companies will continue to be faced with identifying ways to become an employer of choice. Not just how to recruit those skilled employees, but how to reward and retain them. Employee knowledge and skills will be critical in dealing with rapid technological change. HR programs will emphasize selection, "just-in-time" training and development, and tracking of this knowledge and skills mix within the company.

While only a relatively small percentage of the workforce currently takes advantage of flexible work arrangements, it is expected there will be an increase in the use of both flexible hours and work location. The prevalence in use and low cost of the Internet, e-mail and telecommunications technology will make telecommuting easier. Other alternative work arrangements that will increase in frequency include job sharing and team or project-based assignments where one person may fulfill several roles, either simultaneously or via the free agency concept within an organization. Barriers to employing individuals with disabilities are being removed by technology and ability of employees to set their own hours and work environment.

The 21st century will see a continuing focus on the work and family balance issues. Changes in family structure, lifestyle choices and the nature of the work itself will change workers needs and preferences in health benefits. An increasing number of workers will seek benefits that fit a diversity of non-traditional work models, including flexible work schedules and locations, second and third careers and partial retirement.

The emphasis on training and development is forcing companies to look at technology, especially the Internet, to deliver these programs more effectively. Employers will need to ensure their employees are receiving the education and training to keep their skills up to date, training that often must fit outside of the normal 8:00 a.m. to 5:00 p.m. work day.

■ *Technology*

The impact of the Internet and the World Wide Web on the workforce of the 21st century is a given. According to the CommerceNet/Nielsen Internet Demographic Survey published in April 1999, there were 22 million Internet users in the United States in 1995. By 1998, the figure had quadrupled to 88 million and estimates are for 133 million by the year 2000. Given that the Internet is becoming the primary means for distributing information to both the home and the workplace, companies will need to quickly harness this technology.

Speedy access to accurate real-time HR information and the ability to analyze, assess, interpret, manipulate and leverage that information effectively will be key to giving organizations a strategic edge. Successful data mining will be made possible by the use of data warehouses with their ability to consolidate internal and external information and desktop analytical tools.

There will be an increasing use of multiple delivery channels such as the intranet, Internet, and voice response to provide a self-service platform that meets the individual needs of the employee.

The market for application service providers (ASPs) — which provide application and data maintenance on an offsite server with access through clients' browsers — will continue to grow. Having enterprise software delivered over the Internet means fewer resources (time and money) are needed for both implementation and ongoing maintenance.

Self-service will continue its shift from transitional to customized portals that not only allow employees to change their address or W-4 deductions, but also view their 401(k) stock portfolio, read today's business headlines, and make benefit elections based on their job function, status and family situation.

As we move into the workplace of the 21st century with its diversity of people and issues, the human resource programs of the future and the technology used to track, monitor and analyze those programs must be about choice and the flexibility to fit an individual's need and situation.

---

*Lynne Mealy is IHRIM's Chief Knowledge Officer (CKO) leading the development of programs, products, services and events. She is Chair of the IHRIM Boston2000 Conference Committee and a member of the New England Chapter Board of Directors. Prior to joining IHRIM as CKO, she worked at Bank-Boston for 16 years in HR information systems, compensation and strategic management positions. She can be reached at **lmealy@bellatlantic.net**.*

HR 20/20:
Clarifying the View of HR in Year 2020

By Row Henson

Perhaps the only point, on which there is near consensus agreement when looking to the future of HR, is that the corporate organization in the new millennium will be dramatically different than today. Even organizational experts, with widely different points of views on most topics, generally agree that the hierarchical organization of the past will be replaced with a new, less-structured network operation.

This is hardly news to today's HR professional. But changing organizations, which receive considerable attention, are only part of the issue for HR professionals. There are other, equally important forces that will change our future roles. And, the usually recalcitrant HR pro, who might be accused of having been less than ready to embrace change in the past, will simply have to do it. It is that big of a difference and that important for the survival of our function in the future.

What is happening is the interaction of three areas of change, all acting independently and interdependently, all influencing the others, and the combination will drive a change in the role of HR in the first quarter of the next millennium. We are going to shed some light on those changes as we try to improve our visibility of the HR function of the future.

The three areas are a) the demographics of the new worker for 2020, b) the changes in how people will conduct business and what that "business" will look like and, c) the impact of technology.

■ *Worker Demographics*

Who are the workers of 2020? Today they are about six to ten years old. They have been raised in the company of Nintendo games, MTV, and the Internet. They are beyond just being comfortable with the keyboard; they embrace it as a social tool. Good or bad — this generation is already having Web chats with their friends (and in some cases people that aren't their friends).

Because these workers have been using technology since they were toddlers, they will not only be comfortable embracing technology, they will demand that their workplace of choice provide the latest and greatest technology tools because this breed of worker will be able to work from anywhere at any time! They will be very comfortable "collaborating" on projects via the Internet with co-workers they may never meet in person.

These factors may be dismissed by many as simply updates to the new toys of the earlier generations, but the similarity ends quickly. This new generation (Generation N's) have different standards and different requirements. Its members are, for instance, much less dependent on physical contact — face time — in their relations with others. They are almost detached in many ways and have little sense of cause and effect. Their values, their style, and their needs are vastly different from those of their gen-X parents, or their baby boomer grandparents.

> *Those that can marry the energy and innovation of the young with the experience and wisdom of the "old" will have a competitive advantage and an engaged workforce.*

And speaking of the generation Xers, there is also an emerging role for us in the new millenium as well. If the low unemployment rate today is any indication of the future, we will also see a new role of the 50 and older worker. This is the worker who retired early, got bored and now has the opportunity to re-enter the workforce and make a significant contribution — if they have they have the willingness and flexibility to adapt and learn.

In the September 20, 1999 issue of *Business Week* — the bulk of the article deals with "Brain Drain" and the shortage of workers based on a number of factors including baby boomers retiring due to the past bull market allowing many to bail early. Many companies today are looking at ways to keep this experienced segment of the market engaged — including contracts and part-time assignments. One sidebar article was even entitled "It Ain't Over When It's Over." Many organizations are looking at ways to bring out of retirement critical skills to fill the gap as well as programs for transferring wisdom to younger colleagues.

Those are the new demographics with which HR professionals must work and which they will have to increasingly satisfy. They will need to satisfy the demanding X/Y/N worker with technological innovation and bring the Boomer into the next millennium with other incentives in order to supply organization with the ample workforce during this "War for Talent" era. Those that can marry the energy and innovation of the young with the experience and wisdom of the "old" will have a competitive advantage and an engaged workforce.

■ *The New Enterprise Environment*

Businesses, of course, have been going through continual change, with rapid changes in the 1980s and 1990s as pressure for cost reductions, near-term profits, and shareholder value drove companies to flatten organizations and modify working methods. Looking ahead into the 2020 time frame, certain factors of change will particularly impact the HR function.

Almost all companies have become global in their operations with all the resulting issues of language variations, cultural differences, economic priorities, and communications to wreak havoc on the HR organization. The new company is becoming virtual in nature as more employees want flexibility, telecommuting and variable hours. To encourage the new styles of networking, collaboration, and temporary small group project focus, companies are moving towards a wall-less community, both internally and externally. And, around all of that, the competency needs of the company have shifted from physical, hands-on work to where the workforce is becoming intellectual capital for the company with intangible value. It is, therefore, much more difficult to manage using traditional systems and practices.

Collaborative organizations will be much more prevalent — so not only will work among knowledge workers be collaborative, but companies themselves will be the by-product of a networking world of joint suppliers/sellers.

■ *Technology*

If the first generation of technology was supported by host-base computing and large mainframes, managed "data processing" and Client/Server-managed "reengineered work processes," the technology of the future will be about knowledge, collaboration, and the ability to measure the impact of both.

HR Systems will be intuitive and used more by people outside the "HR Department" than those inside. The management of the knowledge worker will require that all "people" managers perform classic HR functions. Technology will enable this function to be delivered to the desktop (or palmtop/watchtop medium of the day). These systems will be about people and for people. Because in the year 2020, service-based organizations will make up 80 percent of the employers and manufacturers will represent less than 15 percent.

The increasing use and improvement of multimedia technology and the increasing pervasiveness of the Internet are beginning to change the nature of HR. For example, we will see increased interviewing over the Internet and the capability for prospective employees (permanent or contingent) to demonstrate their competencies. There will be less of a psychological need for face-to-face evaluation. Much of the company (and HR) communications will be done via this medium.

> *... HR will find itself cast into an entirely new role in the new millennium, essentially in the middle of the dynamic corporate environment.*

HR Systems in the next millenium will publish work with collaborative content necessary for all employees to perform optimally based on their role(s) in the organization. The vendors of the future will provide not only the transactional systems necessary for this infrastructure, but they will become the "aggregators" of content for their customers — and provide a wide range of hosting as the demand for better, faster and cheaper technology support prevails.

■ The 2020 Role of HR

These three factors of change, worker demographics, changing business operation and technology advances, have broad implications for the HR function. As professionals in the field, we must understand three points and implement programs of change, if we are to achieve corporate success in the 2000s.

First, HR will find itself cast into an entirely new role in the new millennium, essentially in the middle of the dynamic corporate environment. Human capital will be the dollars of the future and HR will be the custodian of those assets.

The new role will be that of the Human Capital Strategist, with the responsibility for adapting human principles to business and technology change. The success of the 2020 company might very well be determined by the success the HR function has in getting the right workers with the new technology for the company — and making it work.

Second, the Human Capital Strategist will be required to address the issues of work-life balance for all employees. Whereas, today this is in a transitioning stage, in the new millennium it will be a pervasive employee demand and will impact every segment of the HR system.

Third, the new strategist will need to be deeply involved in guiding and understanding the corporate culture, indeed will probably be the keeper of the culture. The driving force will be the need to attract people who can thrive on the particular corporate culture and grow with it, essentially matching biology against technology, people assets against costs.

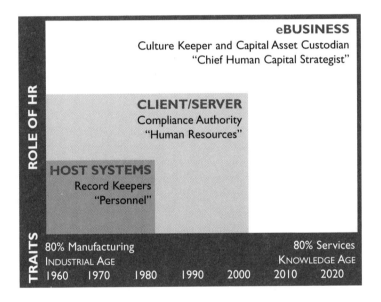

Clearly, the role of HR will force it to be an integral part of corporate ideas, strategies and vision. This will require visibility and participation higher in the organization. We have already begun to see the dissintermediation of the classic role of HR as recordkeeper and legal protector. The "human" side of HR will also be necessary to build and maintain a culture that people want to come to and stay with. It will also be necessary for HR to balance the best of the old school with the emergence of new and innovative practices and supporting technologies to better support this dramatically and quickly changing world. As I have said in the past, HR must get out of the back room and into the boardroom. As keeper of the company's culture and the custodian of the human capital assets, the corporate future might very well depend on it.

Row Henson is Vice President of HRMS Product Strategy at PeopleSoft Inc. where she is responsible for the HRMS product line. She can be reached at **row_henson@peoplesoft.com**.

Consulting in the 21st Century:
Managing the Paradox

By Karen V. Beaman

■ Introduction

> "...the millennium clock of a well-known Swiss company ... promises
> to be Y3K compliant. As well as the usual hour and minute hand, it
> has a year hand that tracks around a spiral scale which has every
> year from 2000 to 3000 marked. What an heirloom for future genera-
> tions of your family, if it still works in 3000! Not to forget, that the
> ever precise Swiss are not celebrating the new millennium until one
> year from now."[1]

I wonder if the new millennium watch will be able to provide us with any
more warning of what Y3K will bring than we had about Y2K? If only we could
consult an oracle or fortune-teller to find out what the future holds... Why can't
consultants help us better prepare for the future?

You've probably heard the joke about the client who asked the consultant
what time it was. The consultant responded, "Give me your watch and I'll tell
you." Consultants are much derided throughout the world; nevertheless, they
fill a vital role in our industry. As illustrated by this joke, consultants help their
clients to see things right before their eyes; however, they also bring different
and fresh perspectives to a situation, helping their clients to see things that
they themselves could not see.

Consulting is one of the oldest professions, going back at least to the time of
the ancient Greeks, well before the Common Era. The Greeks believed that con-

sulting an oracle brought a direct response from the gods. Both common citizens and public officials, for example, consulted the Oracle at Delphi, one of the first known consultants. The natural vapors emanating from the chasm at Delphi, situated on the slopes of Mount Parnassus, were believed to be the voice of the god Apollo.

"The equivocal replies of the Delphic Oracle have become famous in history... they were so obscure... so incomprehensible... that their interpretation was considered as important as the oracle itself. The case of Croesus, the king of Lydia, is a good example. In answer to his question, the god said that if he |Croesus| waged war on the Persians, he would destroy a great power... he never suspected that he would destroy his own kingdom if he fought the Persians. This earned Apollo the surname "Loxias" or the Ambiguous One because of his obscure answers....

"The priests exploited the clients of the oracle. Each visitor had to sacrifice a honey-cake to Apollo. These honey-cakes were sold by the priests. Also, each visitor had to pay for a guide in the temple. Each large city-state or country had its own representative at Delphi. If one's home had not sent a representative, the priests offered locals as guides, for a small fee."[2]

And so, since the beginning of modern times, consulting has been viewed as mysterious, mercenary and even at times dishonest... and, sometimes with good reason. Consultants who don't explain or back up their answers, who don't document their work or transfer knowledge to their clients, and who are intent on nickel-and-diming their clients for every minute of service provide some explanation for why the industry has been saddled with such a questionable name throughout the years.

It is a simple fact of human nature that people do not listen to those they are closest to nor see what is right in front of them.

Yet, consultants serve a useful purpose. As is often the case, an outsider can point out things to a client that an employee or other insider cannot do. This can either be because the employee is so close to the situation that he/she can't see it, or because people generally — and sadly so — put more value on what someone from the outside has to say, especially someone whom they are paying. There is nothing inherently mysterious or dishonest (although you may consider it mercenary) in telling someone the time by looking at their own watch. It is a simple fact of human nature that people do not listen to those they are closest to nor see what is right in front of them.

■ Forces Affecting Consulting

According to the GartnerGroup, CIOs give three basic reasons for using external consultants:[3]

1. Access to specialist knowledge: in general, consulting firms have access to a wider-range of skills, such as leading-edge technology, than does the average organization.

2. Broad experience: consulting firms have experience across a wide range of businesses, enabling them to choose the best solution when working with each individual client.

3. Flexibility: consulting skills are readily and quickly accessible, and the supply of people can be turned on and off at will.

The information technology professional services industry is one of the fastest growing business areas in the world. There are many forces acting on the consulting business and spurring on this growth rate:[4]

➤ Worldwide skills shortage
➤ Growth of the Internet and e-Commerce
➤ Globalization
➤ Economic stability
➤ Outsourcing of non-core activities
➤ Customer demand for a complete solution
➤ Customer relationship management
➤ Y2K lockdown
➤ Advent of the euro (Europe's new single currency)

Some predictions claim that as much as 50 percent of the workforce will soon be made up of consultants, contractors and other contingent workers,[5] all of whom, it should be noted, serve different functions. "Consulting" is quite different from "contracting," and both are decidedly different from what contingent workers do. In consulting, an individual offers specific expertise to "guide" the client through the steps necessary to reach an agreed-upon objective. In contracting, the individual actually "performs" the work, at the "direction" of the client. Contingent workers are temporary helpers used to fill gaps in the workforce. The remainder of this paper will focus on this definition of "consulting" —that of guiding and advising clients in a specific business area — and not on contracting or contingent work.

■ Consulting in the 21st Century

Although the millennium changeover is just an arbitrary date based on the relatively inaccurate Western calendar, it provides an opportunity for reflection and assessment. Just what is it that makes a consulting engagement successful — for both the client and the consultant? And what will need to be different about consulting in the 21st century?

In my opinion, the winning consultant in the new millennium must become a master at managing the paradox. The speed of change and the level of competition are too fierce today to permit companies to pursue a single strategy and stay in the race. Companies need to perform "apparently" contradictory tasks at the same time. They need to have a long-term vision, yet act on short-term objectives. They need to globalize their operations, yet remain sensitive to local situations. They need to capitalize on best practices, yet retain their individual competitive advantage. A valuable consultant is one that helps their clients reconcile these paradoxes and follow multiple, even conflicting, tracks simultaneously, keeping the overall end goal in sight.

Consulting in the 21st century requires a new business model — a business model that is responsive to individual client needs and specific situations, yet all-encompassing in providing standard, rapid solutions to the fast-changing needs of organizations. The new consulting business model must also be flexible and scalable to meet the needs of diverse organizations. It must promote single source solutions — solutions that begin at the visioning and strategic planning stages and that continue though business process improvement, software selection and system integration, encompassing the full system architectural assessment and technological infrastructure implementation as well.

There are six "seemingly" paradoxical capabilities that will be increasingly vital to the successful consultant in the 21st century.

➤ Technical and Functional

It goes without saying that consultants must possess the relevant technical and functional skills. It is no longer sufficient, however, for a consultant to be either the greatest network or database technician on the planet or the most knowledgeable compensation design expert in North America. The successful consultant must be both! Consultants must be able to apply their expertise to the client's business objectives, marrying the functional business need with the technical solution. It is this combination of both technical AND functional expertise that will make a consultant successful in the 21st century.

➤ Generalist and Specialist

In the same vein, consultants now have to be both generalists and specialists. They must have broad knowledge and experience in a wide variety of industries and business functions, but also specific expertise in critical business areas, such as ROI (return-on-investment) analysis, change management, process improvement, workflow automation, the Internet and e-commerce. Expertise in benchmarking and in best practice solutions is becoming increasingly important as companies seek input from their consultants on ways to improve efficiency and productivity, while reducing costs. In the 21st century, the ability to be both a generalist AND a specialist is going to become even more critical to a consultant's success than it is today.

➤ Tactical and Strategic

"Think strategically, act tactically" a former boss once told me, a piece of advice taken to heart, especially in this age of increasing competition in which we have to out think, out plan, and out deliver the competition. Clients want their consultants to help them define the "big picture" of where they are going, but, at the same time, they want immediate results and payback for their investment. Companies are no longer content to dump hundreds of thousands in long-term strategic planning exercises, without short-term deliverables that they can put in place along the way. The

The skillful consultant must balance both global demands and local needs.

consultant of the 21st century has to balance both long-term, strategic objectives AND short-term, tactical solutions to be successful.

➤ Local and Global

While everything we read and hear talks about how globalization is on the increase, there is no question that companies still operate in local communities, with differing legal requirements, cultures, customs and languages. The skillful consultant must balance both global demands and local needs. In *Managing Across Borders*, authors Christopher Bartlett and Sumantra Ghoshal (1991) have called such an approach the "transnational solution".[6] The transnational consultant must master the paradox of being responsive to local cultural needs AND strive for global efficiencies. At the same time, we must leverage and share the experiences we learn worldwide.

➤ Custom and Standard

I've always told our new consultants that if they can't provide their client with at least three options, along with the pros and cons of each, they're not doing their job. Companies want choices; they want custom solutions, tailored to meet all of their specific business needs. At the same time, they want standard solutions that require minimal adaptation in order to effect a rapid implementation and to reduce ongoing maintenance costs. The key to satisfying such seemingly paradoxical client expectations is to provide flexibility — standard solutions that are adaptable and scalable to a variety of business situations — such that clients can have both a standard AND a custom solution, simultaneously.

➤ Open and Proprietary

Over the years, consultants have built up massive knowledge databases, which now contain a wealth of solutions from the company's prior consulting engagements. Clients are now demanding open access to these "gold mines" of hitherto proprietary information, and, for a fee, some consultancies have done this, such as the GartnerGroup and Ernst and Young. But clients are not always willing to pay for this access, particularly when a couple of hours spent surfing the Web can provide much the same information — and for free. Clients are now expecting that this open information access be a part of the standard consulting fees. The paradox for the consultant is in providing such open access to their proprietary information AND, at the same time, protecting the unique solution that gives the consultancy its competitive advantage.

Meeting all of these requirements is a tall order. But no one ever said that consulting was easy. Clients expect more from consultants than they do from their own employees, primarily, because they are paying more for their services. As client expectations continue to increase, so too do our consulting capabilities need to expand in order to keep pace.

■ *Conclusion*

Consultants are both loved and scorned in our industry —another paradox! Client expectations are increasing and consultant capabilities need to grow to meet those expectations. Otherwise, we will continue to be the brunt of even worse jokes (such as, when the client asked a consultant what time it was. The consultant answered, "What time do you want it to be?"). In order for the consulting industry not to be viewed as the mysterious ranting of an oracle or soothsayer, consultants need to expand their reach and embrace the paradox of our times.

Karen V. Beaman is Vice President of International Operations for AG Consulting, a wholly owned subsidiary of ADP, Inc., providing management and IT consulting services for human resources and finance. She is currently the Editor-in-Chief of the IHRIM Journal and a member of the IHRIM Board of Directors. She can be reached at **KBeaman@AGConsult.com**.

■ Endnotes

1   *13 Update (Intelligence — Insight — Innovation)/Entovation International News.* Issue 35. December 1999. David Skyrme Associates Limited (www.skyrme.com) and ENTOVATION International Limited (www.entovation.com).

2   "Greek Oracles: Delphi & Method of Divination." From website: http://members.xoom.com/ ancientwrld.

3   "High-Priced, Arrogant Consultants: A Staffing Solution?" *GartnerGroup Research Note.* J. Furlonger. February 1998.

4   "Western Europe: IT Services Market Forecast and Shares 1999." *GartnerGroup Executive Report.* November 1999.

5   Row Henson. "The Worker of the Future." *IHRIM Journal.* June 1998. Volume II. Issue 2.

6   Christopher A. Bartlett and Sumantra Ghoshal, *Managing Across Borders: The Transnational Solution.* Boston: Harvard Business School Press. 1991.

Remove the "HR" from "HRIS!"

By Sidney H. Simon

We are constantly bombarded today with the concept of employees being the "human capital assets" of the company. As such, who is really the "owner" of these assets? Who should be providing the requirements for managing these "human capital assets?" HR certainly has some claim for the issues they are responsible for, but there are other non-HR issues and other "users" who have a vested interest in these "human capital assets" as well — supervisors, managers, executives and so forth. Although HR believes they may be representing the interests of these other constituents, this can often be debated.

Where is this leading? As noted in the above title, there is reasonable cause to remove HR from "HRIS" — and even take a step further by replacing "HRIS" with "human capital asset management system" (HCAMS). An HCAMS would support not only the HR organization but many other end-users as well. Now back to a prior question: "Who should 'own' or be responsible for the HCAMS?" It is my belief the HCAMS should, in most companies, be owned by the Chief Operating Officer (COO). HR would most likely be positioned in the COO chain of command as well and be a primary user, but HR should not be the ultimate owner.

I believe it is fair to say that today's HRIS/HRIM professionals are basically frustrated in their work — my simple survey isn't highly scientific, but it is good enough for my purposes! We have actually been frustrated for several years, so it is not a new phenomenon. We witness and participate in the technology evolution, which is changing and improving even as this is being written. Yet, we are finding it difficult to use and implement what we know can provide added value to our organizations. Our current primary users and "owners" are unfortunately not changing along with, nor as fast as, the technology. Thus, we are stuck between the proverbial "rock and a hard place" with our work.

My premise has always been to work with and help define what it is the "owner" requires and then deliver it (doing such helps the performance reviews and compensation allotments). User buy-in is obviously essential for the successful implementation of any new HRIS capabilities, functionality and software features. We have continuously heard from our HR user community that they want to be, or even should be, considered more strategic in their participation and positioning within the company. Yet, what have these HR users been requesting over the years from their HRIS teams? Does anything pertaining to "strategic" come to mind? Nothing much jumps out in my mind that is strategic in nature. Certainly, there are some desires for more employee self-service and other functionality for attempting to escape the day-to-day "administrivia" most HR organizations still embrace, but nothing I would consider that demonstrates real strategic or "out-of-the-box" thinking is being requested.

HR users need to look outside of the "HR box" . . . and determine where they can be adding strategic value using the information so readily available to them.

An example of forward thinking and information analysis is a situation I encountered several years ago working on a project for a fast-food company. All stores were still company-owned at that time. The nature of the business involved high employee turnover, which was certainly common in the industry. HR believed approaches were needed to reduce turnover, as their basic assumption was "turnover is costly and affects profitability negatively." The controller also participated, as she needed to provide some relative data and would need to budget any new programs. Out of curiosity, we took the turnover data by store and compared it to the profitability data by store, and YES, as expected, there was a correlation. Strangely enough though, the higher the turnover, the higher the profitability — this was actually not a negative situation as initially assumed by HR.

After digging a little deeper it was determined that when the hourly and part-time workers remained employed too long their wages rose as well, thus increasing the store expenses — revenue however, was not impacted. Training new employees, who were at minimum wage, was not a major issue — managers were expected to spend a lot of their time managing the workforce anyway, so being in a constant training mode was not seen as a negative condition. The controller was thinking strategically here and looking at the business issues at hand versus accepting traditional workforce beliefs. HR never would have taken a different spin on this situation. At least, the project to reduce turnover was quickly abolished. I also believed HR was hoping to reduce their workload by having fewer employees terminate and start on a daily basis, however they never presented any information about administrative cost savings that might be achieved with lower turnover, nor how it would really affect the business!

Unfortunately, I don't recall many similar situations where HRIS data was used in conjunction with financial or other company data in performing a critical analysis. My opinion is the users just aren't aware of what can be done with the data they manage or how to go about it. HR users need to look outside of the "HR box" and better understand what the business is, how it operates, and determine where they can be adding strategic value using the information so readily available to them.

What would this recommended HCAMS transition mean for today's HRIS professional? Once again, in my humble opinion, this would be a major step forward for us. The new HCAMS professional will now be interacting directly on a day-to-day basis with all ultimate systems users and with those responsible for other critical company systems, such as financial, manufacturing and so forth. Such positioning will still enable us to continue to meet HR's basic needs and we would move up several notches by having human capital information used to support more than HR. HCAMS funding and priorities will be set at a higher level in the company based on returns that can be better measured than when left under HR's influence and total control.

...most people in this industry are frustrated with the business "house" and too many are leaving through the "back door" while fewer are entering the "front door."

The next few questions might be: "Is this repositioning for real?" or "Will this ever happen?" or "When will this happen?" If I had to bet on it, I wouldn't put much on the "pass line" for anything happening soon — probably not even in my remaining working life (I have been at this a longer than my youthful appearance suggests)! There may be instances where management understands the big picture and will make some improvements, but "one-offs" aren't what we are talking about here. The International Association for Human Resource Information Management (IHRIM) certainly needs to be providing some leadership in promoting such "thinking" and "behavioral" changes and HRIS professionals must also be somewhat political and proactively seek such changes within their organizations, if this is ever to happen.

And a final question might be: "Am I really serious about this?" First of all, I certainly cannot make any claims about being a major visionary — my stock picks will prove otherwise! What I can say is most people in this industry are frustrated with the business "house" and too many are leaving through the "back door" while fewer are entering the "front door". IHRIM has still not accomplished what were early organization visions (The Association for Human Resource System Professionals (HRSP at that time) to substantially enhance the HRIS profession. Just look around and see how many HRIS "managers" are equivalent to the Compensation manager, the Benefits manager, the T&D manager, the Employment/Staffing manager, and so forth, in a typical HR organization. Everyone will not agree with the positioning issue and that is fine, as long as those people are comfortable with where they are and want to remain there. I get frustrated seeing highly competent professionals losing "the faith" and moving forward in different directions to further their careers. We need to do something about this, so this HCAMS suggestion, as well as others will need to be considered, even though they may appear a little "far out" on the surface — this is a serious situation and radical actions and approaches are needed.

Sid Simon is a founder of IHRIM (HRSP) and its first president. He has remained active in IHRIM, most recently chairing the Edward S. Goldmacher Educational Fund. He has worked in various capacities in the HRIS/HRIM industry including practitioner, software vendor, consultant and services provider. Currently, he is the Director of Professional Services at Cyberbills, Inc. He can be reached at **Sid_Simon@yahoo.com**.

HRMS in the New Millennium:

What will the next 10 years bring us and what is the international perspective?

By Al Doran, CHRP

While I may very well get into big trouble with the very vendors I work with day in and day out in my own consulting practice, just possibly the message I am sending today will be a small wake-up call for those vendors out there who plan to service clients in places outside of the United States of America.

This will not be a new stand for me, but let me back up and explain my position on why I do not think that the HRMS vendors have been doing a great job so far for all of their clients. Later on in this essay, I will take an even stronger stand on the failings of the human resource (HR) community to take advantage of the tools that are available to them.

About six years ago at the Fall IHRIM Conference in Toronto, five former presidents of the then Canadian Association of Human Resource Systems Professionals (CHRSP) were invited to sit on a panel and discuss how HRMS industry had evolved and to predict where it was going. I am not sure if it was luck (bad or otherwise) or if it was by design, but I drew the straw that put me last on the program of the five "wise men." Strange, since I was the only HRMS practitioner of the bunch, with all four of the others, and the moderator, all coming from the consulting ranks.

My four colleagues waxed eloquent about how well the industry was doing, how technology had evolved to the point where we now had easy to use and productive HR management systems and, in fact, we had even better things to look forward to as we approached the mid-point of the 90s and moved towards the new millennium. They did a very good job of it, however one could not help but notice that they were dwelling on the positive and not managing to fit too many of the negatives into their allotted time at the podium. By the time they were through, I suspect that they thought the audience was about ready to say "Let me out of here, I want to run out to the Vendor Expo next door and buy, buy software!"

When my turn came, the moderator indicated we were almost out of time and asked me to kindly keep my remarks to about 20 percent of the time originally allocated. (After all, what could I, a lowly practitioner bring to the table)? Well, I thought I had read this large audience to be comprised mainly of HRMS, HR and payroll managers so I took a shot at it. I said, "Sorry Mr. Moderator, but I think these kind folks have come here today to hear a balanced view of what is happening in our industry and I hope they will bear with us while they hear from at least one practitioner." About that time my pager went off and I held it up and said "There folks, that's the reality of OUR world, we have a payroll problem back at the office so let's quickly visit the facts as a practitioner sees them!"

... the "great lie" that client/server software was going to change our lives, it was going to put productivity tools on our desktops.

That was the closest I ever came to getting a standing ovation. The moderator got the message and sat down.

At that time, I took a poll of the audience to see who had recently implemented or was implementing a new HRMS and many were. Then, I asked if they were finding these systems difficult, time consuming and expensive to install, and they all agreed. Then, I asked if those who had gone live had harvested any major increase in productivity or if any savings had been achieved and the results were discouraging. We could have had a one-hour "bitch session" right then and there as these folks were very unhappy.

I reviewed the promise of the early 90s, the "great lie" that client/server software was going to change our lives, it was going to put productivity tools on our desktops. It was going to enable line managers and functional HR managers to finally have access to the information they needed to manage successfully. At that time in the 90s, very few companies had implemented a new HRMS and seen proof of any of the benefits promised by their vendors. The HRMS remained a "black box" that was only accessed by a few trained technical resources. Paper flow had neither been reduced nor streamlined. On top of that, we could have had another session on just how difficult and expensive it had become to migrate business systems from a mainframe to a distributed client/server environment. Many in the audience related that they were now spending many times more on technical support as they had computers everywhere in the company versus the previous centralized mainframe environment.

One must remember that at that time in our HRMS evolution, we were just starting to hear about workflow as well the Internet, which was just a toy the nerds were using to chat globally. So, the client/server systems available to us then had very little to offer in the way of facilitating how we do our work and how we manage HR information. But, let's be clear, that did not stop the vendors from trying to tell/sell us on the idea that these new systems would change our lives. In reflection, the vendors did a poor job of communicating the facts about their new technology and an even worse job of making sure that we had some tools to work with that would enable us to achieve some degree of success in finding those promised improvements in our business processes.

So, what has happened since the mid-90s? A lot, but in a word, "Internet." The Internet has enabled us to finally gain some advantage from use of the new HRMS the vendors were turning out. Finally, we are able to put reasonably easy-to-use systems on the desks of the people who are entering the information and those who need to access it to make business decisions. Do I think the vendors played a large role in this evolution? NO! They have basically followed along with others who developed solutions and then tacked them onto their systems.

... the vendors have not kept up, and... the solutions they are providing are still too complex and labour intensive to implement.

Almost everyone has attended these one, two and three day sessions on Corporate HR Internets/intranets put on by IHRIM, IQPC, Insight, Canadian Institute, Linkage, Strategy Institute, et al., and heard great case studies and success stories from companies that have developed their Internet/intranet to facilitate employee/manager self service, give access to corporate HR policies, management reporting, etc. But, strangely enough when the speaker reaches the Q&A part of their presentation, they have very strange responses when asked "What HRMS are you using and how have you integrated it with your HR Internet/intranet?" Almost all of the guest speakers relate that they had to go ahead with the HR Intranet/intranet as a separate project as they could not wait for the vendor. This generally means that the vendor does not yet have the "hooks" to integrate or interface with the Net yet, or they are building their own. Sometimes its because the HRMS project has already set the scope of their implementation project and there is no time or resources to integrate/interface with or to develop Internet/intranet solutions as part of the project.

HRMS projects have tended to be large, lengthy, costly and very inflexible in scope. Intranet projects on the other hand have been shorter, cheaper, flexible, and have often produced astounding results in productivity with very low investment.

These responses from companies that have successfully implemented HR Internet/intranet solutions without making the full connect to their HRMS indicate that a) the vendors have not kept up, and b) that the solutions they are providing are still too complex and labour intensive to implement.

◼ HRMS Development — Outlook

Vendors developing new HRMS solutions are going to have to be much more aggressive in developing integrated solutions that combine the latest technologies and bundle those solutions for the client so that large complex systems can be implemented in an integrated fashion. Vendors will be required to spend considerably more time researching the actual business needs of their clients in order to provide the best solutions.

Let's talk about the cost of implementing an HRMS today. Most texts today give a rough guide of "three to eight times the cost of the software license" for implementation costs. It often goes many times more than this. There are claims now that this vendor or this implementation partner can install product X at less than one times the cost of the software license. They are making this claim because they are developing new implementation techniques such as "rapid implementations" which are little more than vanilla implementations where the delivered product is set up as-is and populated with corporate data. There is little history, as yet, to confirm that these claims can be lived up to, and even less follow-up research to track what the costs are after the implementation to tweak the system to work to the point where the client is fully satisfied. The good news is that the vendors and implementation partners are listening; the client is not going to take it any more.

The HR manager who is not computer literate will be long gone before we reach 2010.

Another ray of hope is also shining through for those clients who are unhappy with the trend towards long and costly implementations. Some of the vendors who have traditionally sold to the smaller companies are now marketing solutions that can be a good fit for the larger ones. With the advances in technology, the former LAN-based system for 2,000 employees can easily handle 20,000 employees in a three-tier client/server and Web-based environment. And, they can do it for much less (for the software license) than the competition and they can install the product at a fraction of the cost of the larger systems.

■ HRMS Implementation Costs — Outlook

Vendors are going to be facing a much more competitive arena in both the time it takes and the effort it takes to implement their products. The customer is not going to take as a given that one must pay many times the cost of the software to implement their chosen product. With all the experience gained so far, it's high time both the vendors and the implementation partners have found faster and cheaper ways to implement new systems. Their clients are going to be looking for a positive return on investment (ROI).

■ HR's Role in HRMS

I know, I know, the high cost of implementing these systems is not all the fault of the vendors or of their implementation partners. The client deserves a great portion of the blame due to the fact so many of them are ill-prepared to take on such a major task as implementing an HRMS. Recognition that information management is an important function within human resources has been a long time coming as it's been all to easy for the HR manager to say "let the techies look after it."

An HRMS is one of the most, if not the most, important business systems within a company. People are often the most expensive resource within a company, and therefore, how we manage the information related to them can drastically affect the corporate bottom line. HR managers for the most part are aware of their various disciplines but many of them have not had a great track record when it comes to being able to translate their information needs into business requirements. This is changing slowly as most new employees coming into the HR profession are computer literate and are used to translating their HR business needs into systems solutions. The Internet is also playing a major role in how HR managers are entering the 21st century. Literally every HR manager these days is using e-mail and surfing the Net. There is a new awareness of the need for rapid information and of the many options for obtaining the right information, fast.

As we enter into the new millennium, we are seeing more and more challenges for the HR manager:
a) mergers and acquisitions,
b) globalization,
c) outsourcing,
d) call centres,

e) new legislation, and

f) constant change.

You thought you saw change in the 90s, wait till you see the next 10 years!

The HR manager of today is faced with change on an almost daily basis. HR is still struggling for a voice at the corporate boardroom table, but with an absolute certainty, they will be playing a more critical role in regards to organizational change. The HR manager of the first decade of the new millennium will be faced with providing information to the decision makers that may make or break the company. "Iinformation is power" will be the watchwords for this upcoming decade.

To be able to ensure that Human Resources has the information it needs to manage with, the HR manager will need to know the business of the company and what HR's role is within the company. That has been the weak link for HR through the 90s, with HR not knowing or caring enough to find out what is really needed by the corporation to successfully manage its HR information. Too many HR systems have been "thrown together" without the care and attention to detail that would have assured its success. The HR manager of today cannot afford to say "leave it to the Techies." They are going to have to take the time to be able to understand and articulate their business needs to ensure that the technology solutions chosen are implemented to their best advantage.

■ The Role of Human Resources in HRMS — Outlook

The HR manager of the new millennium is going to have to be much more computer literate than the manager of the 90s to survive. Every HR manager is going to have to be able to translate business needs into automated solutions. The HR manager who is not computer literate will be long gone before we reach 2010.

■ The Canadian Perspective

As a consultant in the business, and one who has participated in many IHRIM and similar vendor shows and expos in Canada and the USA, I have to observe that Canada is short changed when it comes to the number of choices

available to us in comparison to businesses in the USA. There are far more options for core HRMS solutions available in the USA than there are in Canada.
Canada has a few of its own vendors, companies that do not as yet market into
the USA, however, even these are few in number and none of them have major
market share even in their own country.

On a positive note, not all of the USA vendors sell their product line in
Canada. Most of them realize that Canadian requirements differ significantly in
certain areas from USA needs, so they tend to stay away from Canadian sales. I
say this is positive, as there are also a few USA vendors who sell in Canada in
spite of the fact that they have not made a significant investment in making
sure that their products meet Canadian requirements.

There are a number of USA vendors who sell their product lines in Canada
and do so very successfully. These companies tend to have large market share
in Canada and this is due to the fact they have invested the resources necessary
to make their products work in Canada. To keep the business, they also have set
up Canadian research and development (R&D) here and they provide a solid
base of Canadian support to their clients.

One must be careful to not confuse the above "successful vendors" in
Canada with those that just have a "store front" operation here. Some USA software vendors have sales offices in Canada with little or no R&D or customer
support. Those Canadian clients who do not do their due diligence and fail to
fully investigate these vendors do so at their own risk. If the vendor has not fully
Canadianized the product, their clients are in for major disappointments. If that
vendor has not committed to major Canadian R&D and support, then the client
is going to be disappointed sooner rather than later.

A word of caution to those vendors who open up shop in Canada without
making sure their product is ready for the Canadian market, and for those that
have no plans to keep involved and get support from a Canadian knowledge
base, "you're not going to last long."

■ HRMS Solutions for Canadian Clients — Outlook

To be competitive in Canada, HRMS vendors are going to have to work with
Canadians to ensure their products are ready for this market. A Canadian store-
front office will no longer fool the Canadian client; there must be solid R&D in
the back room and there must be strong Canadian support available.

■ International HRMS Scene

For certain countries, the prospect of finding a good HRMS, with adequate support, is even more of a challenge than it is in Canada. In Eastern Europe, for example, it's almost impossible to find good, mature HRMS solutions that are fully developed and supported locally. I have recently been involved in projects in Eastern Europe and it was extremely difficult to find more than a small handful of vendors who were interested in even bidding on projects there. Ultimately, a couple of vendors were found who wanted to establish business in Eastern Europe, however, at that time they had no client base at all and support was originating from other countries such as Germany and Great Britain.

■ Eastern Europe — Outlook

This is an area that is seeing a large number of multi-national companies setting up shop and they are starved for good HRMS solutions. Those vendors who go into this area with software that can be modified to suit local requirements will quite possibly be riding a wave of growth that will last for many years to come.

■ HRMS Globally

With the communications and technology advances greeting us almost daily, we are moving towards a business world where it's going to be expected that we will have to share information in the corporate sense. Those vendors specializing in products that service just one country are going to have a limited audience to sell to in the next few years. Customers are going to want solutions that have the flexibility to manage HR information globally.

Al Doran is President of Phenix Management International, a Toronto, Ontario management consulting firm specializing in HRMS issues. He is a director of IHRIM and of CCHRA and may be reached at **aldoran@pmiHRM.com** *or* **http://www.pmihrm.com/**

Self-service is More Than Y2K Ready

By Michael E. Smith

Is self-service ready for the new millennium? Self-service is a powerful tool offering the potential to reduce costs and bring higher levels of service to employees. From its rather unassuming beginnings of simply using a touch-tone telephone to inquire about a 401(k) balance, self-service advanced in just ten short years to become an essential element of an effective HR strategy. A variety of self-service technologies are now available with features and capabilities that match both the employer and employee needs.

■ *Technologies continue ahead of the implementation curve*

While there always seems to be a steady stream of raw information technology available, workable application methodologies and sound implementation strategies are not always evident. Such is the case with self-service technology and its growing list of accomplishments. For example, interactive voice response (IVR) technology, available since the 70s, took 15 years for its applications and data interfaces to unfold to a point where "off-the-shelf" self-service applications for HR, Benefits and Payroll became readily available.

In addition, the company culture factor reared its head to add a few more years to the process of IVR acceptance. Not that long ago, in TALX workshops one of the frequently asked questions was, "...will my employees really use this?" Now, IVR is universally accepted for employee self-service as well as other daily chores such as banking by phone and tracking retirement plan performance. IVR is also emerging as essential for an effective HR call center or employee service center.

◼ Expectations continue well ahead of the practical curve

When a concept has thoroughly gained acceptance, it becomes one of the prime targets for speculating about the future. And, there are some very attractive predictions these days about what to expect from self-service into the distant future. Some of the common themes include:

... speech recognition technology ... has finally reached a usability factor that is hard to match.

1) Self-service expanding to communicate through smart phones and hand-held personal data assistants (PDAs).

2) Web self-service applications reducing the need for call centers.

3) Employee self-service becoming entirely Web-based.

All of these very possible predictions sound intriguing. However, organizations don't have to wait for these predictions to materialize to begin reaping the benefits of self-service. There are plenty of new technologies, as well as practical applications available today, to build effective self-service solutions.

◼ Will self-service expand via smart phones and hand-held devices?

Without waiting for the complete integration of speech recognition and text-to-speech, organizations can speech-enable some high return self-service applications. While the use of specialized devices, such as PDAs, holds great promise for some self-service applications, a more conceivable communication scenario is the extensive use of speech recognition in the self-service mix. A few years ago, speech recognition made a weak introduction in self-service applications. It was unreliable and too limited in vocabulary for widespread use. Natural speech recognition is one of the most exciting voice technology developments that promises a real impact in the self-service model. This technology has made tremendous advancements in recent years, making it a legitimate self-service technology component.

Today, natural language speech recognition is phonetic-based and allows intuitive applications such as name entry for dependent updates and address entry for change of address updates. Also, rather than drilling through menu forests, which is characteristic of unsophisticated IVR applications, natural language speech recognition lets employees ask something like, "... how many vacation days do I have left?" Simple, but representative, inquiries like this are instantly "understood" and acted upon at once by fabricating concise personal responses.

... it is doubtful that employees will have any more confidence in a Web page than a page from their employee manual.

While speech recognition technology is not to the point where it can support unstructured conversations with an HRMS, very specific applications can be implemented that any employee can use successfully. This most natural of all communication methods has finally reached a usability factor that is hard to match. Employees can now initiate applications very conveniently without using the keys on the phone for menu selections or information entry. The results: shorter session times, ease of use and fewer errors.

Specialized devices, such as PDAs, do make a lot of sense for use with a controlled group of users like managers. A PDA is a good alternative to a laptop for many manager self-service applications and is available at a much more affordable price. Both data and applications can be downloaded to the PDA to guide remote managers through each application. Specialized devices have proven to work well for people in the field for collecting orders and viewing e-mail. There is every reason to expect these devices will meet the needs for basic manager self-service applications.

■ Will Web applications make HR call centers less important?

In the future, call centers may play a less important role, but for now call centers (or employee service centers) are meaningful in maximizing service levels and minimizing the costs to provide service. Additionally, with today's technology, organizations can put in place an HR virtual call center without investing the significant amount of capital required to build a physical counterpart. By outsourcing the call center functions, organizations create their own virtual center that can take employee calls, offer self-service for level 0 for simple queries and transactions, transfer calls to vendors and even connect employees directly to the right department within the organization for complex issue resolution.

Looking more to the future of Web applications, complexity is one of the byproducts of trying to do more and more with Web-based applications. Even though the user interface is simple, "offering more functionality" means employees will present more difficult questions, too. For those important transactions, it is doubtful that employees will have any more confidence in a Web page than a page from their employee manual. Call centers, while smaller, will become even more important in resolving the complex issues.

Self-service technology also is playing an important role in solving this problem. With the addition of IP telephony, employees can get the help they need. Using a "Help-Me" button on the Web page, users can initiate a sequence of telephony and data functions that result in a direct voice connection with an HR specialist. While viewing the same Web page as the employee, the HR specialist can guide the employee through a difficult transaction as well as access a knowledgebase for further details.

Even without the "Help-Me" button, organizations can add a "Call-Me" button that allows the next available HR specialist to call the employee back. Another alternative is to initiate a chat session to get to the ultimate employee issue. Web-based applications will eventually create their own brand of service center needs.

■ Will all self-service applications become almost entirely Web-based?

For some organizations, this might eventually come to pass. But when? For the overwhelming majority of organizations, self-service access must be balanced to reach all of the potential users. Choice is a key factor in meeting employee expectations and needs. Not all employees have intranet access for self-service applications.

The best employee-facing implementations tend to be those that offer support for multiple technologies. As a result, employees can use the phone when it is convenient and use the Web when transactions require a full keyboard and visual access. In some cases, IVR is an important backup technology when the network is not available and a time-critical transaction must be completed, like benefits enrollment or payroll reporting.

■ Creating a tailored self-service solution

There is a rich mix of self-service technologies available today. Even though these viable technologies and proven applications are ready, a bigger question remains — how will these self-service capabilities be delivered to an organization's HR, benefits and payroll departments? In addition to the option of an organization building its own solutions, three other popular delivery options should be investigated.

➤ Self-service via HRMS vendor
First, a self-service strategy can be built upon the solutions offered by the HRMS vendor. In support of the "all Web-based" applications theme, most HRMS vendors have a product strategy to integrate self-service applications using Web technologies. This option is maturing as some vendors are even on their second generation of products. This approach is appealing because the self-service solution comes from the same vendor that delivered the HRMS.

With the HRMS-delivered approach, all employees access the HRMS through a browser at the desktop or Web-kiosk to create self-service transactions. However, it is important to take into account how to support those employees who cannot access the intranet. Also, take a close look at the company culture in terms of the Web-only model.

In following the course of using an HRMS vendor-provided set of self-service applications, all of the HR, Payroll and Benefits information needs to be located in one central, integrated database. Such an approach works for some organizations. But for many organizations, all of the information needed for self-service transactions is not contained in a single database. Consider carefully, too, which applications the HRMS vendor has developed. Do they match established priorities? When tailoring applications or building a new one, an organization needs to become proficient in using the tools the HRMS vendor selected to build the core self-service capability. These tools need to be evaluated in view of the organization's web application development direction.

➤ Server-based self-service
Next, a design approach that seems to offer the most flexibility is to base the self-service applications on a separate server. This server-based alternative con-

figured with self-service applications software can support interfaces to established databases so multiple applications can be implemented. With this approach, applications can be matched to needs rather than taking what is given.

Self-service servers are available from companies specializing in self-service implementations. Generally, these servers are designed from the ground up to support all of the required self-service technologies initially identified and for future applications — including options for HR call centers. Taking into account some of the future devices like PDAs and smart phones, an organization more likely will find support for these devices coming from a server-based solution.

Self-service is certainly ready right now and well-positioned to support the growing need for high quality employee services.

Speech recognition, "screen pops," faxing, and e-mail capability can be activated, as needed. In addition, a self-service server has the capability to build or create applications in an open environment. This scheme also fits the need to implement central workflow to guide employees and managers through complete business processes or access the HRMS-supplied workflow system.

This option also offers the flexibility for complete solutions to be implemented, with or without significant internal IT resources. The commitment of internal resources requires training and ongoing involvement to stand ready for the next application or upgrade. However, if an organization prefers using internal resources exclusively, core support is generally available for all self-service technologies not just web applications.

➤ **Outsourcing self-service**

And, finally, with the speed of technology evolution and the resulting high investment essential for information technology solutions, many organizations are looking at outsourcing as a viable alternative. A new breed of outsourcers called application service providers (ASPs) are matching the needs of the many enterprises. This is because the ASP is focused on setting up the desired business applications, not just the computer and network infrastructure. Outsourcing is once again a popular option as organizations consider their core competencies. An enterprise focus on outsourcing has arrived at the same time that self-service is coming of age. Now, organizations can consider outsourcing their entire self-service application suite.

Outsourcing self-service is not a new concept since most organizations have long ago outsourced their 401(k) or other defined contribution plan administration. An indispensable component of the outsourced 401(k) recordkeeping role is the self-service functionality such as balance inquiry, transfers and loan applications. And, now, this same concept is easily expanded to enable HR, payroll and other benefits self-service applications to be totally outsourced.

This may sound good, but perhaps the organization wants all self-service transactions to be made instantly, online to their integrated databases. Today's communications technologies don't limit access to only the batch file transfer model for data exchanges. Frame Relay can be used to tie outsourced self-service applications directly online to the organization's integrated databases. This allows instantaneous access to all business rules without replication. Updates and transactions can also be stored immediately in database tables, ready for immediate access and processing.

Today's self-service technologies require significant IT resources for implementation. If information technology resources are readily available in an organization, then creating applications internally may be a wise choice. While the return on investment is good, even a modest self-service initiative does require a capital investment to get started. If an organization is not prepared to make a capital investment, outsourcing might be the best alternative.

Once a desired set of self-service applications is defined, each should be considered separately for insourcing or outsourcing. Many applications, such as employment and salary verification or benefits enrollment, can be selectively outsourced to minimize the initial technology and staffing investments. In fact, outsourcing the first application is one of the quickest ways to begin realizing the advantages of self-service.

The self-service predictions made for the years to come portray a strong future for self-service implementations. Whether or not the current predictions are realized to the full extent, there is ample technology and capability to move forward today and be successful with a self-service initiative. And, to help realize all of the benefits of self-service, several viable delivery choices are available when setting up a "packaged" or tailored set of applications. Self-service is certainly ready right now and well-positioned to support the growing need for high quality employee services.

Michael E. Smith is Vice President, Business Development for TALX Corporation. He is an IHRIM member and frequent speaker and author on the application of self-service technology. He can be reached at **MES@talx.com**.

Succession Planning in the 2000s

By Ren Nardoni

For organizations faced with more demanding leadership requirements in a changing, more competitive business environment, the installation and use of a new process for succession planning may be the most important human resource management investment they can make. This process, which may or may not need to be supported by a computerized succession planning information system, can provide benefits that go well beyond the traditional reason for succession planning, which has always been "to assure the continuity of leadership at the top." Today's reasons for having a formal, data-rich approach to succession planning include:

➤ The basic change in the "social contract" between employers and employees — a result of downsizing and other factors — which has had the effect of diminishing managers' long-term commitment to careers aimed at top management positions,

➤ Reorganizations, mergers, and management "flattening" efforts that have disrupted existing success planning "ladders," often eliminating jobs that were traditional stepping stones to the top,

➤ Changing organizations moving into new lines of business, new globalized markets, or new technology, which demands new types of managers with different qualifications, skills and talents,

➤ Any organization that believes in career development for all or most managers and professionals — the 90 to 95 percent of managers who "feed" succession planning's candidate files — requiring an approach that motivates employees to succeed and helps the organization prepare future business leaders, and

➤ Companies where the reality or perception of "cronyism" or discriminatory practices affects the career commitment of an increasingly heterogeneous management cadre, necessitating an approach that defines qualifications for all to see, and provides a framework for fair succession.

These "new" reasons for succession planning often require consideration of a computerized system to handle extensive data and automate procedures, but first the "process" involved in succession planning needs to be defined by the organization.

■ Defining the Process

One way to define succession planning is to describe it as "career planning at the top," an extension of the principles and procedures that the company uses to merge the career aspirations of individual managers with organizational goals and management needs. This view is accurate, in one important respect, because both career planning and succession planning are (or should be) "developmentally oriented," focusing on the long-term development of managers for future positions and specific activities — training, education, experience, and so on — that prepare managers.

But, because succession planning typically focuses on the five or 10 percent of key positions in the organization that are considered critical leadership posts, and because these positions often have different requirements than all other management jobs, succession planning usually requires a separate or additional set of "position requirements." The skills and talents required to lead key functions, business units, or the organization as a whole, are not necessarily the same as those needed at intermediate or specialized management levels. For example, the job descriptions of plant supervisors or data processing managers do not usually call for an understanding of global economics or competitive marketing strategies. Thus, a separate system for key leadership positions that is more than a mere "extension" of career planning is usually in order.

> *... a separate system for key leadership positions that is more than a mere "extension" of career planning is usually in order.*

Position requirements are one of the three main components that define a succession planning process — and may require extensive data applicable only to "key positions" in the organization. In larger organizations where 50 to several hundred key positions are covered by succession planning, detailed job descriptions and text that spells out the requirements of leadership positions are often best handled by computerized position files in a succession planning system.

The second component of succession planning is the "people data" requirements. Also, these are usually more extensive than career planning for the obvious reason that positions at the top of the organization are more critical to business success and more should be known about managers in line to succeed to these positions. For example, a career planning system might incorporate data from performance appraisals that simply rate a manager's performance on a one to five scale. Data on potential company leaders should be more extensive and detailed, explaining the reasons for the rating and providing an overall context for the appraisal. Leadership positions may also suggest the need for expanded biographical information — such as a candidate's service in community or fundraising organizations — that is not necessarily relevant in other HR systems.

The more extensive data requirements of succession planning systems and the fact that it covers individual people at the higher levels of the organization, provide yet another reason for creating a separate process and, when warranted, a separate system to support the process. That reason is security, specifically personnel data privacy. Much of the "expanded" data on individuals in a succession planning system is information

... this system ...
lends itself
to politically expedient
privacy procedures
and access limits.

others in the organization have no real "need to know," such as personal biographical information or details of a performance appraisal. And, the fact that this system is one covering the organization's most influential leaders, lends itself to politically expedient privacy procedures and access limits.

The third main component defining succession planning is development activities, which link people and their qualifications with the requirements of key positions. Like position requirements and qualifications in a succession planning system, developmental activities also are likely to include different, and sometimes unique, types of information and activities that usually go beyond activities carried in a career planning system. For example, a career plan targeted on domestic marketing positions may not need to include education or experience in dealing with foreign governments or offshore production: A potential CEO or international marketing V.P. would need this experience or knowledge.

■ Impacts of Downsizing

The first of the "new" reasons for creating and installing a structured approach to succession planning in modern organizations is the disruption caused by the dominant corporate employment trend of the 1980s and 1990s: management downsizing. Reductions in force at management levels throughout the organization, sometimes called the "flattening" of hierarchical structures, has typically had all or most of the following consequences:

➤ Management positions at the headquarters level, traditionally "stepping stones" to the top, have been eliminated, often through reorganizations and decentralized staff functions to the field or outlying business units.

➤ Middle management positions across the organization have been permanently restricted out of existence. Some became redundant after a merger or acquisition, some have been replaced by decision-support technology, and others simply fell to the need to reduce the costs of doing business. Whatever the rationale, however, the management positions are "gone," reducing the management opportunities available to all employees.

Companies can no longer take for granted that the quality managers they need at the top will emerge from a vast reservoir of aspiring managers in the lower ranks.

➤ Individual job security has eroded with downsizing, outsourcing, decentralization, and other ways of "doing more with less" in the management ranks (including the introduction of technology, though this does not always have the desired effect on headcount). Today's managers and professionals no longer expect to have lifetime careers with their current employers, changing the fabric of traditional career planning.

➤ The traditional "ties that bind" employees to employers — compensation and benefits — are further weakened as not only are there fewer management positions, but those that remain pay less in total compensation. Companies will continue to seek ways of controlling benefits and "total compensations" costs — through participatory health insurance plans, limits on pensions, the use of temporaries, part-timers, and contract employees who don't receive benefits and other measures.

All of these and other cost-cutting trends of the last decade or so are continuing today, and these trends have helped contribute to the employment environment known as "the new social contract" between white-collar management employees and the companies they work for. On the employers' side, the new environment means less needs to be spent on "care and feeding" issues in human resource management; for employees, the results are often a predictable decline in company loyalty, commitment, and a willingness to put the goals of the organization ahead of their own personal and career interests. With a few exceptions, the "organization man" of the 1950s has been replaced by men and women trying to balance their work lives with family concerns, and people who expect less from their employers in terms of careers, security and fringe benefits.

The dilemma this poses for organizations with a growing need for experienced, dedicated, increasingly specialized managers and professionals is obvious. Companies can no longer take for granted that the quality managers they need at the top will emerge from a vast reservoir of aspiring managers in the lower ranks. The "quality" managers that once emerged because of the "quantity" of managers competing for top jobs are no longer assured.

At the same time, the demands of upper-level managerial and professional positions have escalated. Technical skills unknown to the "generalists" of the past may be required. Business and financial skills have become more complex and new issues in the global economy need to be understood and managed. To identify, nurture, and retain quality managers in today's environment, more and more organizations are turning to formal succession planning and the data-intensive computer systems that support it.

■ A New Process Helps Underscore New Goals

Another reason for the development of a new succession planning system — with new job requirements and different standards of management excellence — is the powerful effects succession planning can have on changing corporate culture and management strategies. When an organization is "changing direction" for some reason, and has different needs for management skills, new business objectives, and different strategic objectives, a new succession planning system built on these new criteria of leadership helps support and implement change.

For example, a company with a new strategic mission as an organization — say, diversification into new lines of business or expansion into global markets — can introduce a new succession planning system that clearly identifies the new requirements of key positions. Managers are not only "told" that the company now values new skills and knowledge — such as an understanding of a new line of business or international marketing skills — they also see that their future as senior managers depends on the acquisition of new capabilities. And, when the succession planning system is incorporated with developmental activities, as discussed below, managers have both the motivation and the means of preparing themselves for the new requirements of future positions on their career paths.

The development of new managerial job requirements, development activities to help managers acquire new abilities, and other characteristics of a succession planning system can also become a "proactive" strategic undertaking in changing organizations. If long-range strategic plans call for a different type of manager five or 10 years from now, succession planning and its development activities can assure that managers know what will be expected of them in the future. Specific skills such as fluency in a foreign language or the ability to use a computer system can become part of management development today, assuring the future availability of these skills.

When individual aspirations don't "match" organizational goals or needs, the individuals should be looking elsewhere for career fulfillment.

New criteria and standards used in succession planning can also support efforts to change an organization's corporate culture or way of doing business. One major employer, for example, added entrepreneurial skills to its "dimensions of leadership" when it expanded into new markets requiring more aggressive, competitive management behavior. Others in today's "quality conscious" environment might add job requirements that reflect the importance of product or service quality in leadership positions.

■ Succession Planning as a Driving Force for Development

When a succession planning approach is "conceptually integrated" with other management staffing and career development programs, the staffing goals "at the top" can permeate the entire organization, and serve as the driving force for all career development and staffing systems.

Conceptual integration means that the terms, skills definitions, values and frame of reference for two or more systems are consistent. The idea of what constitutes relevant work experience, what "quality" means, technical and professional qualifications, performance measurements, and all other fields of information that two systems have in common mean the same thing to all parties — both the managers covered and the management users of the systems.

When succession planning's concepts, goals and terminology have been accurately formulated — based on the real needs of the business and strategic plans — these concepts can and should be incorporated in career development systems covering the 90 percent or more of managers who are not yet covered by succession planning, or all in the organization who may at some time in the future be candidates for key positions of leadership.

The advantages of this consistency are more than administrative. The high visibility of succession planning and its position requirements serves to motivate those covered by career planning and development. In large or complex organizations with many business units or dispersed locations, all managers are working toward the same career and organizational objectives — which in an effective career development program are closely aligned. (When individual aspirations don't "match" organizational goals or needs, the individuals should be looking elsewhere for career fulfillment.)

◼ A Tool to Eliminate Discrimination

Another reason for installing a formal succession planning process and a mechanized system to support the process, is to provide a framework for the elimination of discriminatory practices in top-level promotions. The system itself will not stop discriminatory practices or unintentional perpetuation of "the old boy network," but some of the key components of a formal succession planning approach provide a *modus operandi* for avoiding cronyism in selecting corporate leaders.

Cronyism, of course, is defined as the appointment of one's associates to responsible positions "without regard to qualifications." A main component of any succession planning approach, and a key set of files in a computerized system supporting succession planning, is the definition of "qualifications" or job requirements for each position covered. When these qualifications are spelled out in advance, known to all participants in the process, and made the basis of development activities designed to prepare managers for succession, selection committees and others who actually pick successors have a much harder time picking their friends "without regard to qualifications." This drive towards objective criteria does not, however, negate the importance of "soft" criteria needed to balance the executive work team and provide for the appropriate "chemistry" necessary to optimize success. The long-term view should attempt to minimize the soft requirements and accentuate the objective criteria.

More, well-intentioned managers responsible for selecting candidates and promoting individuals have clear-cut guidelines to follow instead of "hunches," or the kind of unconscious discrimination that can afflict promotion practices.

In many cases, the mere definition of what the qualifications are for a certain top-level position helps eliminate unintentional bias. When the developers of a succession planning approach are defining the requirements of key positions and putting it on paper, the genuine qualifications of positions are much more likely to emerge. Does it really matter what college this candidate went to if she has this qualification? Are ten years of service with the company a "qualification" for this position, or is this a requirement we could do without? Why couldn't a person in a wheelchair hold this job? And, so on.

> *Succession planning . . . can contribute to employees' morale and sense of the company as both "a good place to work" today and a place where "effort pays off" in the future.*

In operation, of course, the succession planning system with its clearly spelled out qualifications for key position, provides a framework and methodology for selecting the "most qualified" successors. Whatever the true qualifications for any given position are, and whatever weight the company decides to give different qualifications, these factors can be part of all succession planning documentation and communicated to all participants.

Finally, the very existence of a succession planning system used to identify candidates, identify position requirements, and support decision-making can help avoid the "appearance" of cronyism in the top management selection process. Reality is what matters, of course, and it is a safe assumption that any organization willing to put the time and effort into management development and succession planning intends to get the full benefits of an objective, fair approach to promotions. But, in an increasingly diverse work force, where the commitment of more women and minorities at all levels of the organization is increasingly critical to success, widespread understanding or the company's merit-based approach to top management selection helps create and maintain employees' commitment to their jobs and careers.

Succession planning is, after all, just an extension of career development — the "top slice" of an approach and system that covers all managers or even all employees — and as such, it can contribute to employees' morale and sense of the company as both "a good place to work" today and a place where "effort pays off" in the future.

Ren Nardoni is the founder and principal of ClearView Consulting which provides a variety of human resource and information technology consulting services. In 1984, he founded Nardoni Associates, Inc., internationally known for succession planning and 360 assessment software. He can be reached at **Ren@clearviewconsulting.com**.

HR Self-Service in the 21st Century

By Miriam Ward

Human resources professionals can expect radical shifts in the delivery of employee services as we move into the 21st century. Administrative and employee service functions will ultimately be handled with greater efficiency and effectiveness through use of modern call centers and mature self-service applications. Seeds of change were planted during the 90s, although self-service pioneers have not yet fully delivered the employee and managerial self-service applications suggested by HR visionaries.

Customer-focused process improvement trends of the late 20th century readily led to ideas of using technology to improve customer service. Human resource leaders began to consider moving transaction processing close to the source and using merging technologies to deliver information directly into the hands of employees.

While early endeavors have been successful in delivering some basic transaction processing directly to employees, these limited transaction based applications are a far cry from the full potential of comprehensive self-service human resources applications. The capacity for employees to handle personally their own transactions, such as changes to their address or W-4 deductions, was initially provided by some corporations via interactive voice response (IVR) and corporate intranet applications. A shift to using Internet Web browser technology to deliver human resources self-service applications is becoming more widespread in both public and private sector institutions as we enter the 21st century.

Such self-service applications, while exciting to the organizations that have invested significant resources in the deployment of self-service transaction processing, tend to provide employees with little more than a view of their data and an opportunity to update certain items linked to pages of reference text. The evolution of self-service will witness another generation of self-service that provides far more than basic Internet read/write transactions.

Self-service in the coming decade will expand to include customized presentation of information regarding human resources programs, policy and benefits. As employees access their organization's self-service, they will receive both personalized details that answer specific inquiries and also the opportunity to conduct personalized transaction processing. Customized delivery of human resources programs, policy and benefits will be available as individuals access employee self-service applications via the Internet. A customized profile based on data in the corporate human resources information system (HRIS) will provide the basis for delivery of this pertinent information. No longer will an employee need to read pages of summary plan documents or sort through paragraphs of generic policy or contract language in an effort to determine what rights, rules, benefits and services apply to him or her. A unique "cookie" created and stored during the secure browser session will serve as a filter to ensure appropriate information profiles are served to the inquiring employee.

Multiple navigation options will be available, enabling employees to easily access what they want to know. An employee will be able to navigate, view and process any human resources information or services based on life events, services desired or other defined categories. No longer will Internet information be provided by locating the web page of the organization or department offering a service. Rather, self-service offerings will welcome employees to click into personalized information based on what they currently need to know.

Avoiding information overload and quickly providing concise and accurate, personalized information will be a primary objective of self-service.

Life event choices, including beginning employment, family changes, job changes, education or health changes could direct an individual to information needed at a point in time; whereas an employee may know specific services desired and prefer to link directly to information on a unique topic. Sophisticated search engines will be available to connect an employee to the information needed without selection of endless Internet clutter on any given topic. Avoiding information overload and quickly providing concise and accurate, personalized information will be a primary objective of self-service, if it is going to be successful in replacing personal interaction with human resources staff. However, self-service applications will also need to link to some centralized customer service center in order to provide the human element when necessary for assistance with self-service or to answer unusual inquiries.

A new breed of data content management tools will be available to HR systems professionals to provide means for companies to simply create and maintain consistent up-to-date information displayed on hundreds of self-service web pages.

Employees are not the only ones who will see radical changes in services via the Internet. Managers can also expect significant change in how they administer and handle employees using Internet-delivered managerial self-service applications. Hiring authorities will initiate requisitions in minutes and have immediate posting of jobs via the Web. Imagine, within minutes of receiving an employee's resignation, the manager is able to create an open requisition to replace the individual who resigned. Moments later the position is posted and available worldwide via the Web. At the same time e-mail messages or computer telephone messages are automatically being sent to individuals who may be interested, qualified candidates, specifically inviting them to apply for the open position. While this is occurring, other potential applicants are submitting applications via the Web and are being self-screened as likely prospects for the position. Hiring processes that once took days and even weeks may well be accomplished in less than 24 hours by the end of the decade.

Self-service design will also need to recognize that an individual may have multiple roles within the organization. An employee will require access to their company's employee self-service for personal reasons and because that same person is also a manager or supervisor, quick and convenient access to managerial self-service is also needed. Having a personalized web home page whereby a person may establish links to preferred self-service offerings as well as other Internet services and e-Commerce will provide the convenience necessary to make self-service offerings desirable. Employers will offer options for initializing and maintaining personalized portals whereby an individual can set up their own web home page to most fully support their current roles, interests and needs.

Hiring processes that once took days and even weeks may well be accomplished in less than 24 hours by the end of the decade.

Traditional 20th century security solutions will not suffice in the new era, and security issues will continue to challenge both developers and a generation of increasingly sophisticated hackers. Increased layers of security will include increased utilization of private key access. Access will be authenticated through use of private key security loaded on each individual's computer or using portable card readers to read swipe card computer chips. While futurists look toward retina scanning or fingerprint security access, it is not likely these security measures will be widely deployed in the first decade of the 21st century. Whatever the security solution, we can be sure the importance of highly secure applications will be imperative to ensure full acceptance of self-service via the Web.

Imagination, service need and technology will come together to deliver a powerful new means of providing information and processing to the workforce in the coming decade. HR systems professionals will be challenged not only to develop new self-service offerings, but also to identify deployment methodology that recognizes the human element for accepting change in the 21st century.

Miriam Ward is a past president of IHRIM *and a 1997 Summit Award winner. Currently, she is Director of* HR Information Services *for the University of Minnesota. She can be reached at* **wardx022@cafe.tc.umn.edu**.

Compensation Systems for Tomorrow

BY RICK OLIVIERI

A lot of the compensation "old timers" (people doing compensation for 25 years or more) are fond of saying that there have really been very few new developments in the compensation field. Being an old timer myself, I believe they are mostly right. Except for some new design concepts like broadbanding, competency based pay, and some features of executive compensation (primarily due to legislative changes), the compensation programs of today are pretty much the same type programs your father designed.

There is, however, one facet of compensation that has changed tremendously: the tools used to design and administer compensation programs. To give you an example, 25 years ago all surveys were completed using paper and pencil. Participants of compensation surveys gathered their input data from COBOL paper reports generated by the IS organization, after many meetings and trial runs to ensure you got the right data, calculated correctly. If that wasn't enough fun, you then took the data from that report and laboriously transferred it to a paper survey form using a #2 pencil and then snail-mailed it to the survey sponsor. Behind the scenes, the survey sponsor would transfer the data from yours, and every other survey participant's input sheets onto graph paper, and start the process of calculating average salaries. Of course, the calculator used was pretty primitive compared to the ones used today. Because of this, most survey sponsors didn't do more than calculate average salaries back then because it was so difficult to calculate anything else.

Even the median salary (which is a better compensation measure than average) was difficult to calculate because you didn't have a means of sorting the data from high to low once it was copied to graph paper. Needless to say, the average salary rates we're given to a secretary to type using a new electric typewriter. Hopefully, the typist was a good one and didn't make too many mistakes, because you had to backspace to the mistake and type the mistake again while inserting a little white paper into the cartridge and then type the correction. Many times, whole paragraphs had to be redone in this fashion, or started over. Because this process was so labor intensive, most of us tried to only pass over for typing, final hand-written materials. Lastly, the typewritten materials were copied, probably using mimeograph and mailed to the survey participants, and the survey was completed. Needless to say, there wasn't a lot of good survey data back then.

Thankfully, the times have changed. Compensation professionals can now get most of the data they need through direct access to the human resources database or by someone in human resources creating an extract for them, usually in Excel, Access or something similar. This data can be cut and pasted into templates or compensation people can literally construct the desired format and do your basic V-lookup using Excel to combine the template and the data.

... the tools and process of doing compensation will become so efficient that it fundamentally will change the way we pay people.

The majority of survey data is now submitted by diskettes, e-mailed or entered into a web site. The survey sponsors can upload the participant data into their software and manipulate the data to their hearts content. Consequently, we now get not only median data, but percentile pay rates. Even the average data is more accurate, because survey sponsors, in many cases, now collect individual person data. So, instead of getting average company data average, you get the actual average salary for all individuals represented in the survey. For the participants, data can still be accessed by paper, but more often now it is accessed through electronic files sent via e-mail or via the Internet by compensation professionals. These electronic files also make it easier to analyze the data and apply the results to the particular organization. In addition, you can change the data by changing the sample of participating companies you want to look at. You can merge the data with your own and calculate the percent difference. You can construct graphs showing the average difference by salary grade or job family. You can cut and paste this data onto a PowerPoint template in order to make a presentation using a LCD projector.

I think you get the point. A great deal of paper and labor has been eliminated from the survey process. And, the data is better and much easier to analyze and communicate than in the old days. Just in case, you haven't been convinced yet, let's take a few more examples. Does any compensation person remember how to calculate a regression line (primarily used to analyze data for engineers, attorneys, and executives) by hand? I don't either, however, I do remember spending a half-day, or so, to sum columns of numbers to get the formula. Then, doing it again to check the first results. Heaven help you if you came up with a different answer the second time, because then you had to do it a third time. Now, we have programs that can calculate a regression formula in the blink of an eye, and provide you with additional data like standard deviation to help you determine the reliability of the formula. And, it's always right.

How about this one? Ever try to calculate a new salary structure by hand? It would take a day to get just the right midpoint progression to cover all the salaries with the right range spread — and with the right number of grades. Again, programs are available today that would allow you to model hundreds of salary structures in a couple of hours. Here's one final example. We used to model stock options to determine the potential gain of a grant to an executive several or more years into the future. If there were lot's of executives and/or multiple grants, this process could take days. Now, we have programs that will allow us to determine how many shares will be vested on any given date and the value of those vested shares given any assumption you would want to make about future stock appreciation. It might even give you an estimate of the taxes that would be paid should they be exercised. Elapsed time, about five minutes.

... there no longer will be the need for other job evaluation methods .... Every job will be market priced.

OK, enough about yesterday and today. What about tomorrow? If the past 25 years are an indication of the changes we can expect in compensation, it will be interesting indeed. In fact, I believe the tools and process of doing compensation will become so efficient that it fundamentally will change the way we pay people. Let me make some predictions.

First, the compensation professional will have access to much more survey data than is available today — with all of it online. A company's jobs will be matched to survey data by discreet skill set components. Thus, each person's job will be somewhat unique when it comes to analyzing market data and, therefore, more accurate. The major skill components each individual possesses that is used in performing their job will be identified and stored in the company's human resource system (e.g., strong skills in basic statistics, writing skill equivalent to 12th grade, medium knowledge of basic accounting procedures). These skill sets will be compared to other people in the market place with the same required skill sets in order to determine the marketplace compensation. This process of matching company individual skill sets with market data will happen automatically on a continuous basis. Electronic agents will be constantly scouring the cyber marketplace for new data that matches the company's individuals, adjusting the data for geography and size of company, and then downloading that data into the human resources database for later viewing.

Because of this change in how marketplace data is gathered, it will change how compensation is administered in a company. Since every person has a specific, required set of skills to do their job, which can be matched to similar skill sets in the marketplace, there will no longer be "unmatchable" jobs. Thus, there no longer will be the need for other job evaluation methods such as point-factor, factor comparison, whole job ranking and the like. Every job will be market priced. Also, since every individual has a somewhat unique set of skills, each person will have their own current, customized compensation range. By the way, these ranges would be made available to manager's real-time in order to more accurately relate pay levels to individual performance. Therefore, there will be no need to construct or maintain a company-wide salary structure. Also, there will be no need to maintain a corporate list of legitimate job titles since employees would be categorized by skill sets for comparative or analytical purposes. All these changes would be possible, because individual skill sets could be developed and maintained using the appropriate software along with the greater emphasis on the Internet as a medium to collect and analyze data.

> *Some individuals*
>
> *may choose to spend*
>
> *their dollars*
>
> *for an enclosed office,*
>
> *more vacation days,*
>
> *less salary and more stock.*

Due to more sophisticated human resources and payroll management software, we may begin to see the use of "total employment flex systems." These systems would allow compensation professionals to assign dollar values to each component of employment, including stock, bonus, salary, insurance, vacation, training, etc. Each new hired employee would be given a total employment dollar (or credit) amount based on the level of work to be performed and expected performance. The new hire could then allocate these total employment dollars in any way he/she sees fit depending upon individual needs, level of risk orientation and motivation hot buttons. Some individuals may choose to spend their dollars for an enclosed office, more vacation days, less salary and more stock. In this way, compensation and the rest of the employment contract can be customized for each individual employee at hire-on, and adjusted appropriately through the years at the company. This type of compensation system will not be possible without good computer software to analyze the worth of each facet of employment and ensure that all company programs are tracked and paid correctly for each individual. The use of a "total employment flex system" would be a radical departure from the corporate systems now used to attract, retain, and motivate a workforce.

Finally, I think we will begin to see the emergence of true expert systems that managers will use to help them manage their people. These systems will provide managers with advice on how to handle people-related issues. In the compensation area, hard data such as an individual's pay level, skill-set and performance data will be monitored and analyzed constantly by these expert systems. They will also collect and analyze market information as well as internal data such as the pay and performance levels of comparable internal individuals, company and business unit goals and financial performance, human resources policies and program parameters and precedent actions. In other words, these systems will be able to take a much more holistic approach to an issue or problem and provide advice to a manager after considering many variables — by voice, of course. They will, therefore, replace some of the more routine advice and consultation now provided by compensation and other human resource professionals.

In summary, most of the changes we see occurring in the compensation area, up to today, have been due to the insertion of computers and software into the compensation process. They have made compensation professionals much more efficient, but they have not changed significantly the way people are compensated. However, in the next 25 years, computers, software and networks will become so robust that they will change fundamentally the way people are paid and how they work — all for the better.

Rick Olivieri is the Director, Compensation, Benefits & HRIS for Adaptec, Inc. in Milpitas, California and has more than 20 years experience in designing, implementing and administering compensation programs in the corporate and consulting world. He is President of the Bay Area Compensation Association and on the HR Advisory Council for San Jose State University. He can be reached at **ricko@corp.adaptec.com**.

In the Year 2025

By Paul J. Piper

In the year 2025, we're likely to be living and working in a vastly changed world and the youngest HR professional of today will be in charge. What will it be like? How will businesses be organized? How will living standards, work processes and global trends change our world?

Several new influences will have evolved and changed things forever. Over the last 40-50 years, the automobile created the suburbs, air travel and shipping created global businesses, and television created branding and mass marketing. Looking forward, the Internet, telecommunications, genetic engineering, and smart products promise to change just about everything yet again.

■ We won't see the "Jetsons," but the changes will be profound nonetheless.

Let's examine George and Maria's imaginary day in the year 2025 and see how different things might be. It's not a "Jetson's" world of transport and magical kitchens, but the changes are profound nonetheless. Events, technologies, and adaptive social evolution have determined the course of change. I've tried to personalize this future vision and kept away from preposterous "imagineering" — with the possible exception of my vision for HR in 2025 and beyond.

■ *Meet George, Maria and family in the year 2025*

George and Maria Gadea get up early these days to prepare for their day. George puts on the coffee and begins to prepare breakfast while Maria checks the laundry to be sure the children's clothes are ready for this Monday morning. Their two children have to get up early so they have time to dress, eat and get off to school. The day starts much as it has for many decades, but we do notice a few important differences from when George and Maria were growing up.

First of all, the laundry took all night to dry since they use a new technology which dries the cloths quite slowly by a process that saves nearly 85% of the energy used in earlier gas or electric dryers. Sounds a bit like a step backward, until you consider that electric costs are rising by 10-15% per year and have been since 2020. Second, the children will be walking to a neighborhood school less than five blocks from their home. George and Maria remember when they were young and had to ride a bus for over 25 miles to school each day. There are lots of differences in the school programs and some public schools have begun experimenting with at-home schooling using an interactive satellite education system for most of the week with the two days spent actually at school devoted to physical education, music and art, as well as laboratory classes. It saves energy costs and young families like the flexible schedule.

> *Virtually, the entire globe is electronically connected by the year 2025 in a variety of ways with ultra high-speed video and audio networks.*

■ *Global contract services dominate with more people working from home.*

George doesn't drive to work anymore as he and Maria did years earlier. Before he is even dressed, he signs on to his communicator screen and checks the work assignments and scheduled conferences and training sessions for the day. George works for a worldwide technology support company and does nearly all his work from home — diagnosing problems and communicating instructions for local people to carry out. His company is the third largest technology services firm in the world — the two largest global companies are also in the contract services business. Maria works outside the home at night at the school where their children go each day. She is a freelance language instructor teaching Spanish and English to about a dozen adults in the evenings. She also instructs a number of large adult language classes during the day, using her communicator screen. Basically the programs are self-taught, but she listens in and coaches students who need a little help.

■ *Language becomes a competitive differentiation.*

Language skills have become extremely important career skills for many people, especially technical workers since most businesses have significant global operations and markets. George speaks several languages including English, Chinese, and German and of course, he grew up in a Spanish speaking family. Ten years earlier, George's employer provided him with several years of language classes as well as technology training. That's where George met Maria. While English is still an important worldwide business language, worldwide competition has driven many global firms to commit to doing business in the local language in order to compete on a level playing field with local firms. While international mega-mergers seemed to be the answer decades earlier for firms to buy their way into local markets, it became very expensive and difficult to find job candidates. The GE and ABB local acquisition model for global growth (GE's Jack Welch exhorted his managers to act locally, but think globally) of the late 20th century was supplanted by cooperation among global services firms and manufacturers since global communications had changed so much.

■ *Interconnected networks on a global scale*

Virtually, the entire globe is electronically connected by the year 2025 in a variety of ways with ultra high-speed video and audio networks. The World Wide Web of the 1990s has grown into many interconnected networks on a global scale, with technology solving the compatibility problems and access choices automatically. Many people now wear designer earpieces and glasses connecting them to their networks throughout the day. New homes are typically equipped with large wall sized screens for communication — both personal and business. It's hard to find differences between developing and developed nations when we look at the elite, technology savvy people around the world. But, unfortunately there are vast numbers of people lacking these technical advantages, primarily due to ignorance or a lack of education. The younger people have jumped into technology head-first, often leaving the older generation in the cold.

■ Soaring energy prices and the growth of village communities

Today, Maria will go to a meeting 30 miles away driving their electric vehicle. George and Maria own two vehicles, but generally they use their electric vehicle, keeping it charged up in their garage. It travels about 300 miles on a charge and it takes about two hours to charge. It is much more economical than their gasoline engine vehicle, since the cost of gasoline began rising so quickly since 2015. The cost of gasoline in 2000 dollars is now about US$18 a gallon, and it's still rising by nearly 10% a year. Much of this cost increase represents taxes enacted to reduce pollution and forestall projected shortages.

It's not the typical big city environment of the 20th century — it's more like a village center where they live.

Five years earlier, the Gadea's decided to move to a community where they would not need to travel by car as far or as often. Shopping is close by and deliveries are made simple by ordering what they need using their communicator devices. They travel by vehicle to meetings, social engagements, and cultural attractions, but generally they walk or bike around the village. It's not the typical big city environment of the 20th century — it's more like a village center where they live.

■ The environment is extremely important.

Pollution problems peaked worldwide around 2015, with the developing nations spewing out enough air pollution to choke the whole globe, and the developed nations finally recognizing that they had to change their ways to help the world survive. George and Maria purposely try not to purchase anything that involves a lot of wasteful packaging, and since online retail doesn't depend as much on packaging to advertise and push their products, this helps to reduce waste and garbage.

Big issues are nuclear and chemical waste disposal which is still a growing problem, and, of course, pollution prone industries. It's been easy to convince people to reduce garbage and to drive their vehicles less, but industrial polluters are still a worldwide problem.

■ *Racial and cultural differences are less of an issue in 2025.*

The business and employment picture hardly takes notice of racial and cultural differences these days, since color and creed aren't apparent in the electronically connected world of 2025. In fact, George and Maria considered buying their home in a Spanish speaking neighborhood, but opted for a more mixed neighborhood. While people are moving into cluster neighborhoods, the big cities of old appeal more to the older generations who are not as comfortable with the electronically connected world. The real gaps in society are between the young and old, the technically educated and not well educated. This trend is worldwide and promises to disappear in a few more decades with continued emphasis on technical education and training in all countries.

■ *Global government regulation*

Recently, some of the major countries of the world relinquished much of their sovereign powers to world government organizations in order to deal more effectively with worldwide problems. The key issues included: industrial pollution, inter-country electronic privacy policies, world energy conservation, regional military defense, international air travel, international monopoly and trade regulation, and patents and intellectual property protection. This was a big step and an important one, which will clearly take decades to solve requiring nearly all nations in the world to join the movement. The United Nations, as it was chartered, had little real authority and no way to follow through in dealing with these issues in such an interconnected world.

George and Maria were supportive of these political changes understanding how important they were on a worldwide scale — after all, they had close relatives in several Latin American countries and their children were growing up in America. Nationalism is beginning to be viewed as a worldwide obstacle in solving these global problems. Electronic voting and electoral campaigning, beginning nearly two decades earlier, gave George and Maria the opportunity to participate in these political changes with their votes and their opinions communicated as never before possible.

■ Services dominate products.

The world has become very affluent in products and conveniences, at least for the educated portions of the population in most countries. Fifteen years earlier, George and Maria began to recognize that they needed fewer products to clutter up the household, but they needed more and better services to support their lifestyles — energy, waste disposal, economical transportation, reliable high-speed global communications, recreation, education, and myriad household and business services. George and Maria's jobs are in the services area as are more and more jobs worldwide.

■ Loose corporate affiliation rather than employment

The idea of joining a single company and commuting to the workplace each day characterized the previous century, but does not reflect the norms of the 21st century. Working at home, commuting as little as possible, and using your employer to help you find contracts is the norm in 2025 for more and more people. Flexible employment is the trend. Flexibility in work hours, compensation, benefits, training and affiliation are the keys. Those employers who understand how to attract and retain people by continually providing training, rewarding work contracts, and compensation and benefits that fit the skills and quality provided by the individual are the ones dominating world business. It's too easy for employees to learn new skills and technology and move to new pastures.

Maria is strictly an independent contractor and George has stayed with his employer because they continually provide him with rewarding service contracts and the ever-needed technology training that keep his skills sharp and in demand. George's firm has been rapidly growing for decades and specializes in distribution technologies using a wide array of technology and innovation. The firm contracts with manufacturers worldwide for its services.

▪ HR is transforming and becoming the driver of global business processes.

For a while in the beginning of the 21st century, it looked like HR was doomed to be a necessary, but unimportant part of most major business enterprises. But, as technology became more widespread and competition for skilled workers escalated, the HR function took on more importance especially in the midst of globally interconnected businesses. Senior management saw HR's role as key in managing diverse workforces with loosely affiliated employee populations and growing dependence on services. HR is now responsible for relationships rather than employees, and their objectives are finally aligned with corporate goals. Fewer and fewer people in management and efficient electronic communications enabled HR to transform their corporate role. In 2025, HR has begun to manage relationships with contractors, service firms, employees and customers. It turns out that in this new electronic world, it is the human touch that differentiates and guides the rapidly growing organizations.

> *The question is not do we need HR, but rather, do we need line management?*

George's contact with corporate is generally through the HR group, since the concept of line and staff management has blurred so much. Intelligent and consistent policies tempered with flexible and innovative hours, compensation, benefits, and training are what make the electronically connected organizations grow and prosper. George likes the way his organization works. His co-workers and his managers (though there are fewer of them) are readily accessible and approachable. He looks to HR for guidance in dealing with relationship issues, be they with others in his organization, his customers, and other firms as well. HR schedules George's work assignments and training activities. HR is no longer in the background simply writing policy manuals, advising line supervisors, and counseling employees about their benefits. HR is now a composite of marketing, management and staff support. The question is not do we need HR, but rather, do we need line management? The modern corporation is a set of relationships more than it is a group of employees, or bricks and mortar, or even a brand or product.

Yes, organizations abound in 2025 that are structured as they were in the 20th century. But, the trend is now clear and the electronic organization is like the quality movement of the late 20th century, with innovative HR groups leading the way for prosperous new companies.

Sound preposterous? Not really — someone needs to assume the lead in this new business landscape. Will it be line management, marketing, finance, HR or just visionary CEOs? My guess is that the leader will take risks and get dirty. HR needs to re-define their role and mission, and it needs to be far more than record keeping and head counts to lead organizations into the 21st century.

Paul J. Piper is a Principal with IBSC and a member of the IHRIM Board of Directors and has been an active member of the Mid-Atlantic Chapter for many years. He is founder and past President and Chairman of Business Information Technology (BIT), an HRMS consulting firm. He can be reached at **PJPhere@aol.com**.

Managing Human Capital in 2014

By Ruth Ladner

Karen Parsons, vice president of human capital for Bracken Corp., stepped out her apartment door and followed the long corridor to the monorail, en route to Bracken's local office cluster. The company had instituted these clusters many years earlier — even before cars were officially prohibited from entering the inner city in 2010 — to ease recruitment difficulties and in support of voluntary initiatives to minimize pollution from commuting. Ten employees shared Parsons' particular cluster, where they had access to videoconferencing, teleputers, and the collegial contact that simply was not available in home offices.

Arriving at the cluster, Parsons opened the secure front door by placing her palm on the biometric security device. She said hello to "Otto," the Office Tele-computing/Teleconference Organizer, which reminded her of her 4:00 P.M. videoconference with executive management. She proceeded down the corridor, stopping when she reached the first empty office. There a retina-scanning device automatically detected her identity and signaled the door to open. Immediately, the lights came on, the room's climate controls were set to her preferred settings, and the desktop system brought up her home portal.

Parsons' mood this morning was somewhat nostalgic: she was celebrating her 25th anniversary in the field of corporate human resources. She reflected on how much things had changed since 1989, when she'd started out as an HR specialist in a big *Fortune* 500 firm. In those days, she'd done little more than help employees fill out forms and push papers through the bureaucracy.

◼ *Big Picture Replaces Paper Pushing.*

Parson's current job entailed much more analytical thinking. Mundane tasks could be handled automatically, enabling her to look ahead to anticipate the company's future HR needs and to focus on employee well-being. After all, that's why she'd been interested in HR in the first place: she enjoyed finding the right staff member for the right slot, and now she had the tools to do it on a continuous basis. The company benefited because the employees' productivity went up when they felt more energized, engaged and interested.

In recent years, Parsons had faced the interesting challenge of helping to manage a unconsolidated organization. She dealt with issues such as building a corporate culture and engendering a sense of belonging in a geographically dispersed workforce. There was no question that technology had played a big role — especially the advanced HR management system — but knowing when the human touch was required was still important.

In the past, Parsons had been able to search only for specific capabilities and past work experience. Now the software also highlighted candidates' areas of interest, aptitudes and potential.

Well, work was work, no matter how much she'd come to enjoy it, and so far no one had invented a way to get it all done automatically. So, Parsons called up her calendar on the teleputer in front of her and turned her attention to the day ahead. Her most pressing concerns were reviewing employees' benefits choices, projecting and fulfilling her division's HR requirements, and bringing executive management up to speed on the state of the company's human capital.

◼ *Benefits Become a Breeze.*

A quick glance at the benefits overview on her teleputer showed Parsons that all the employees who were due to revise — or reconfirm — their benefits choices during the open-enrollment period had met the deadline. The current HR system's "push" technology was a tremendous improvement over the traditional method of chasing people down to make sure they signed up. Now workers were prompted to register, alter, or confirm their benefits preferences during the designated time period.

Thanks to the built-in wizard that coached employees to select the assortment of benefits that would serve them best, she'd only had to field one or two out-of-the-ordinary questions throughout the entire enrollment period. It was nice not to have to do too much handholding. It left her more time to focus on the big picture.

Parsons thought that one of the more unusual benefits choices Bracken employees had these days was deciding how often to get paid: daily versus bi-weekly. A number of workers could not resist the tangible results of seeing their money accrue in web dollars at the end of each business day, but the majority were willing to wait two weeks for the funds. It was interesting, really. The offer of daily payment was a clear carrot to job candidates; however, once on board and confronted with the tradeoffs as depicted on the company's HR portal, most were content to give up instant gratification in exchange for the enhanced benefits package designed to entice them into leaving their money in the company's coffers for as long as possible.

■ Staying Ahead of the Curve

The benefits review quickly concluded, Parsons turned her attention to the more strategic activity of projecting upcoming resource requirements. An important part of her charter at Bracken Corp. was looking at the whole scope of the enterprise, noting potential personnel problems and opportunities at the corporate, division, department, group and individual level. Parsons not only kept informed of the company's key goals, she was responsible for shuffling competencies to ensure that the goals were achieved. Usually that meant fishing in the corporate pool for appropriate talent, but she was always prepared to throw her line elsewhere when in-house talent was scarce.

Scanning the graphic depiction of the human resources tied up in the company's eight active projects, Parsons discovered that the A Team chart showed warning levels. Drilling down to the relevant details by clicking on the bars in the chart, she noticed that the team was on its third consecutive high-profile project. She looked closely at the individuals involved. Five out of seven had been with the group through the last several projects. One was a new employee. Another had transferred recently from the C Team because her skill set matched that required for the A Team's current project.

Of the six who'd been at Bracken Corp. for some time, three had not taken a vacation in the prior 12 months. More telling, the stress levels recorded at their quarterly in-office checkups were registering unacceptably high. Clearly, these employees needed to take their scheduled vacations soon. She would see that the A Team was shifted to lower-priority projects for the next two rounds. She flagged each individual employee record with a cautionary note, so that, should an employee transfer to another group for a specific project, his or her situation would be immediately recognizable to the new team's manager.

The A Team's manager, Jack Murphy, was somewhat of a superstar himself. Parsons knew she'd have to address these issues with him personally. No doubt, he'd carp about the lower-intensity projects — and maybe even about the enforced vacation time. But, he was an intelligent man, and Parsons had the facts at her fingertips to back up her recommendations. Murphy would quickly see that shifting into lower gear for a project or two was far preferable to burning out his talented team — and possibly losing some of them completely if they were driven by exhaustion into jumping ship.

■ Assembling the Right Team

At the opposite end of the spectrum, Team B was about to take on a demanding strategic project, the success of which the entire company was banking on. In preparation, Parsons and the team manager, Liz Payne, would need to somewhat revise the team make-up. Parsons called up the list of skills she and Payne had worked up along with the inventory of team competencies, vacation requirements, and several other factors, and set out to locate the necessary team members.

The team requirements took the form of a matrix of characteristics weighted by significance. Running the matrix through her system, Parsons came up with a list of current employees who could contribute significantly to the impending project. Because Bracken Corp. subscribed to several external recruiting sources, the system also listed external people who could handle the project and might be interested in making the move to Bracken.

The lists of current and potential human resources were ranked by their suitability to the project: 98% match, 97% match, 92% match, etc. Gazing at the list, Parsons was reminded of the first time she had used a search engine to research information on the Web. Then, the technology had seemed very advanced. Now, it resided in a desktop tool she used every day and was so familiar that she took it for granted.

■ *On the Prowl for Talent*

Parsons was pleased to see that she could reallocate existing Bracken Corp. personnel to cover the key new project, so it wouldn't be necessary to hire. Nonetheless, she studied the list of suggested nonemployees. Parsons made a practice of regularly reviewing available — or potentially available —workers, particularly those in the engineering, sales, marketing and customer-support arenas. One never knew, and it was far better to keep a tab on the pool of job candidates than to have to scramble at the last minute when the company was in dire need. The candidate descriptions she reviewed were mostly anonymous, likely belonging to people who already held jobs in other firms but who saw the wisdom in keeping a discrete eye open for promising career alternatives.

The system also enabled employees to track the results of suggestions, reinforcing the precept that their input truly mattered to the company.

The most recent release of her recruitment software included a nifty new feature, dubbed "soft skills." In the past, Parsons had been able to search only for specific capabilities and past work experience. Now the software also highlighted candidates' areas of interest, aptitudes and potential. Based on individual goals, past performance, education, and other factors, the software evaluated the candidates' ability to handle programming languages, design tools, test equipment, and other technologies that they hadn't studied in school or with which they had no on-the-job experience. This greatly broadened the pool of potential candidates and, even better, helped Parsons hire enthusiastic employees who were truly interested in their jobs and who viewed Bracken Corp. as an avenue to career advancement and job satisfaction.

Of course, with modern-day telecommuting capabilities and Bracken's office clusters, Parsons was not limited by geography. Indeed, these days the world was her oyster when it came to seeking prospective employees.

Aside from the opportunity to work on projects that suited their own particular interests, the increased enthusiasm of Bracken employees could be attributed to a number of sophisticated HR practices that had been incorporated over the years. Parsons felt, for example, that the new "suggestion box" capability yielded significant advantages. Unlike its traditional counterpart, whereby employees simply recorded suggestions, the contemporary suggestion box enabled Parsons and her colleagues to analyze the suggestions, spot trends, fulfill key employee requests, and detect opportunities for making the workplace more appealing to both existing employees and recruits. The system also enabled employees to track the results of suggestions, reinforcing the precept that their input truly mattered to the company.

■ Briefly Briefing the Executives

After a lunch break in the food court near the monorail station, Parsons returned to the office cluster, this time pleased to nab an office with a better view than the one that she inhabited in the morning. Addressing her home portal, which had appeared on the teleputer in front of her, she said, "Videoconference." The desired window appeared on the screen, and Parsons verified the participants for that afternoon's executive conference.

To prepare, Parsons worked with the HR system to create two conceptual views: real-time ("What do we need to do right now to meet our HR requirements?") and simulation ("What can we do to maximize capacity in the coming year without causing undesirable fallout?"). She mused about how her HR work had become so much more analytical than transactional. Now, she could spend time thinking about how people worked, how she could help them grow to be better workers, why certain job functions existed and how they could be made more useful, how potential human resource shifts would affect salaries and related expenses, and, therefore, the bottom-line — all the questions that had been extremely difficult, if not impossible, to answer in the days before effective HR software models.

She was buoyed by the realization that she had time during her workday to ponder the future, rather than helplessly waiting to be ambushed by it.

Shortly before the videoconference was due to start, Parsons spent a few minutes freshening up in the lavatory. She was back in the office in time to see a number of windows suddenly appear on the teleputer, each containing the image of one of the executives. Her mind flashed back to the videoconferencing systems companies had tried to use in the late 1980s. She marveled at the improvements in quality, speed, and bandwidth, which had transformed the technology into a useful day-to-day tool.

In the old days, meaningful HR information was harder to come by, and she dreaded these conferences. But, today she handily fielded questions such as:

➤ "Do we have the human resources we need to handle the several major potential projects we hope to win?"

➤ "How difficult would it be to staff up for the Bright-Star initiative? How expensive? Can we do it? Can we afford it?"

➤ "If we go ahead with the Joi Rae International acquisition, how will the addition of human capital affect the rest of the company?"

The speed with which the HR system enabled Parsons to assess these questions meant that she could even handle some unexpected queries on the fly.

Her prowess made her smile. How far the tools had come since she'd started out in this business.

Of course, her knowledge of her craft was useful, too. One had to ask the right questions in order to come up with the right answers. Parsons believed that the competency seminar she'd attended the previous fall had helped hone her skills, besides giving her the chance to mingle with some of her peers in related industries.

■ *On the Right Track*

The briefing completed, Parsons spent the rest of the day reading articles on the future of HR: she believed that the pioneering work in teleporting would one day revolutionize employment and HR practices. She was buoyed by the realization that she had time during her workday to ponder the future, rather than helplessly waiting to be ambushed by it. That thought, as well as the gratification of a successfully completed executive briefing, made Parsons feel good about her 25-year HR career and the prospects for the future.

She thought, "Not a bad career, HR. When I got into it, I really had no idea how interesting and rewarding it would turn out to be — even aside from all the high-tech tools we use today." However, thinking for a moment about trying to complete everything she had done that day without the tools HR professionals had come to rely on, she shuddered involuntarily and gave the teleputer a grateful pat on her way out the door.

Ruth Ladner is Senior Vice President of Genesys Software Systems, Inc., the Methuen, Massachusetts-based provider of outsourcing services and software applications for human resource (HR) management, payroll and benefits. She can be reached at **rladner@genesys-soft.com**.

The Six Levels
of HRIS
Technology

JOHN SULLIVAN, PH.D.

Most people are aware that the use of technology is expanding at an incredible rate. However, few people have attempted to classify the expansion of human resource information systems (HRIS) into an easy to understand pattern. Are HRIS expanding in a linear pattern or are there quantum leaps ahead? Last year a team of experts from Cisco systems, McKinsey Consultants and myself conducted an exhaustive analysis of the future of HRIS. The following is my summary of the results of that effort.

■ Level # 1 — Paper-based legacy systems

Initially, all HR systems were paper-based. Rather than being designed all at one time, most HR systems evolved gradually with features added, as the need arose. Unfortunately, this meant that most HR systems were lacking in logic and they generally integrated poorly with other paper-based business systems.

■ Level # 2 — Early PC technology

Independent PC-based or local area network (LAN) systems were developed independently and were based on the paper-based systems they replaced. The HR database was accessible only to HR specialists (and not to managers). The outputs of these early systems were primarily written reports that categorized or "just listed" people-related information. Advances included databases that integrated with payroll and rudimentary versions of applicant tracking. Tesseract, ABRA, HR2000 and Greentree are systems representative of this period.

■ Level # 3 — Most HR paper systems are transferred to electronic database systems.

HR systems began to have an HR department-wide impact and to integrate with other enterprise-wide systems. Most systems were still just "fast file cabinets and report writers." In most cases, the software was written to mirror the old legacy paper systems. PeopleSoft, Restrac, Resumix and SAP were adopted by a few HR leaders while others bought separate, independent systems for each HR sub-function.

■ Level # 4 — HR systems are designed to automate transactions so that HR can focus on becoming a strategic partner.

"Doing transactions well" became the focus of most HR technology. Call centers became a basic low-tech option. Some firms by-passed call centers and shifted directly on to intranets, kiosks and self-service. The rapid growth of ERP's forced the integration of independent HR systems with most other business systems. The majority of systems are still not Web-based. HR "owns" and continues to selectively distribute people-related information. Report writing is still the primary role of HRIS. Peoplesoft and SAP become common and Web-based applications begin to emerge.

THE BEGINNING OF THE HRIS REVOLUTION — THE SHIFT AWAY FROM "INFORMATION"

The 21st century signals the beginning of the dramatic revolution in HRIS. Instead of just continuing to automate paper based legacy systems, HRIS vendors must begin to break the mold. Rather than just " dumb databases," HR systems must begin to become " intelligent" as the focus shifts from providing information to HR professionals to that of giving information directly to managers in order to improve the quality of their decision-making. In short, HR systems must shift from the role of "just providing information" to the new paradigm of actually improving the quality of the decisions that are made by individual managers!

MIS people have known for years that merely providing information does not automatically improve the quality decision-making. In order for decision-making to actually improve, HRIS must provide the following:

➤ the right information, including forecasts and environmental data,
➤ just the right amount of information must be provided,
➤ an expert system that walks them through in a step-by-step format,
➤ a format that is desired by the user,
➤ available on a self-service basis,
➤ from anywhere, 24 hours a day,
➤ just before/ as it is needed, and
➤ there must be a "learning" component that changes the recommended action based on past successes and failures.

GLOBALIZATION AND "THE WEB" FORCE THE END TO MOST "FACE TO FACE" HR

Most U.S. firms are just beginning to learn how to manage "remotely located" people. As the trend toward globalization continues, it is becoming more and more common to have workers and plants located in facilities miles from centralized HR. As telework (either working at home or on the road) increases, fewer and fewer employees will be located at any corporate worksite.

Under the old HR paradigm, managers and employees relied on face-to-face contact to get most of their answers. However, cheap and easy Web access has caused the shift in the model away from people and towards Web-based, desktop solutions. The shift is illustrated as follows:

CHANGING
HR TECHNOLOGY
PARADIGMS

■ Old Paradigm: PERSON / PHONE / DESK

When you had a problem you tracked down your local HR representative to get the answer. If you couldn't find them you called to get the answer and if all else failed you looked it up on your hard copy desktop manual.

■ New Tech Paradigm: DESK / PHONE / PERSON

Under the new technology paradigm when a manager or an employee has a problem they will first attempt to solve it themselves using self-service Web-based tools that are available on their desktop or their laptop computer. If an answer is insufficient, they call a specialist, either at a call center or at a shared service "center of excellence." If they need more individualized or advanced information, they would talk to a generalist who specializes in advanced problem solving.

Most firms have found that, although there is some initial resistance to losing their "own" onsite HR generalist, both workers and managers eventually grow to like the use of technology much the same way people have learned to use ATMs instead of tellers at their local branch bank. As customers become more accustomed to using technology, they will demand that it permeate everything we do. And although it is often seen as a "soft" function, HR will not be exempt from this trend.

■ Level # 5 — Systems designed to increase individual manager and worker productivity begin emerging.

New capabilities will begin to emerge in functional areas that previously were largely ignored. Systems will begin to emerge that help managers identify and eliminate complex problems like retention; others will help forecast upcoming issues like labor strife, and some will provide new mechanisms for delivering HR services, like remote learning, on the companies' intranet. In addition, complex decisions like compensation and skill assessment that previously could only be made at the corporate level can now be successfully delegated to line managers with no loss in decision quality.

Other Level 5 tools that will increase a manager's productivity include:

➤ internal databases in HR will be linked to other internal business databases (sales, production, market research) to help HR identify the impact that future business needs will have on the HR services we offer,

➤ early smoke detector "predictors" that will help managers to identify problems before they get out of hand,

➤ early " sprinkler systems" that will rapidly provide information and possible solutions to minimize or mitigate any damage just as problems break out,

➤ "push" e-mail technology that will auto-send customized information directly to employees and managers just as they need it and in the form they like best,

➤ all tools will be Web-based, global and available 24 hours a day, and

➤ the intranet will become the primary mechanism for delivering HR services and information through the "self-service" model.

THE FINAL FRONTIER — EXPERT SYSTEMS THAT PREDICT AND "LEARN"

■ Level # 6 — Smart systems that "learn" and increase their predictive/forecasting power as they are used.

When HRIS finely breaks the "bonds" of paper legacy systems, it will transform itself into one of the most beneficial functions in the entire business.

■ Advanced HRIS Systems Will Allow Us To Shift Most People-Related Decision-Making Directly To Managers And Employees.

There are many reasons why firms need to use HRIS to increase the manager's role in people issues. They include:

... the intranet will become the primary mechanism for delivering HR services and information through the "self-service" model.

➤ Allowing managers to make most HR decisions gives them "ownership" of their problems and their people issues. Technology allows HR to provide managers with an easy to use system with enough information and tools so that many managers actually enjoy making people decisions.

➤ Managers are closer to their people problems and their "customer" than is centralized HR. If managers are given the right information and tools, they are likely to make better and faster decisions than any centralized HR function could.

➤ Managers, like athletes, atrophy (weaken) when they don't exercise their decision-making skills. Managers must make tough decisions on a regular basis in order to maintain their mental "muscle tone." It weakens managers when they are allowed to avoid the toughest decisions of all, which are people decisions! A lack of practice in making tough people decisions makes managers indecisive in other important decisions relating to product development and resource allocation.

Centralized HR decision-making confuses workers as to whether "their" managers are real decision makers or if they are just "let me check with the HR department" people (where HR is the real decision maker!). This also allows managers to "blame HR" for business failures because the managers were "handicapped" with little control over people matters.

■ Here Come Expert Systems.

Rather than just providing information and reports, HRIS will develop systems that actually (and measurably) improve the speed in the quality of the people decisions made by managers. The characteristics of these "expert" systems include:

➤ *They utilize multiple databases* — Advanced databases will draw information not only from within the different functions of HR that themselves draw from other business functions (such as sales, finance and marketing), but also from external economic databases and forecasts.

➤ *Expert systems (analytics)* — "walk" managers through every step of a decision about people issues. Expert systems use "decision trees" to gather information at every step of the decision process. Because the information that is provided varies depending on how the manager answers previous questions, there is no need for advanced training. Probabilities are also provided so that managers know what risks are associated with each decision.

➤ *Mass personalized/customized delivery* — Intelligent systems that learn about the information preferences for each individual manager so that the HRIS system can mass customize/personalize the amount, the format, the timing and the type of information and the services it provides in order to fit a manager's unique situation.

➤ *Systems that learn* — as HRIS systems are used, successes and failures are fed back into the system so that the system "learns" and modifies its recommendations based on experience.

Centralized HR decision-making confuses workers as to whether "their" managers are real decision makers or if they are just "let me check with the HR department" people (where HR is the real decision maker!).

➤ *"Predictor" algorithms* — anticipate and forecast possible problems down to the individual employee level in areas such as turnover, recruiting, pay and employee relations.

➤ *Integrated databases* — Internal databases (performance management, surveys, workforce planning, sales) are integrated with external databases (economic, industry, supplier and customer) to increase the effectiveness of HR planning.

➤ *"Sprinkler systems"* — are developed to automatically minimize the damage done when a major HR problem occurs (sexual harassment, violence, strikes etc.)

➤ *HR effectiveness* — is measured in an overall HR index that focuses on speed, impact on employee productivity and profit increase.

➤ *Market forces (fee for service)* — and "service level agreements" force HR to switch its service mix to fit a managers needs.

➤ *"What if" scenarios* — and virtual reality simulations allow managers to try out ideas and to test different scenarios in order to make better decisions? Competitive Intelligence (CI) databases (if-then scenarios) allows CI systems to show the probable reaction of our competitors to proposed business decisions in order to anticipate and " preempt" their possible moves.

➤ *Online simulations* — These can be used to aid employee training and candidate assessment.

➤ HR's role shifts from the distributor of information to that of consultant and coach on only the most difficult people issues. HRIS allows managers to become self-sufficient for most HR issues.

■ Conclusion

From putting paper systems on a computer to the development of expert systems that anticipate, learn and mass personalize the information they provide is certainly a giant step. However, if HRIS professionals are to remain leaders in business decision-making they must evolve from "information providers" to professionals that provide the people closest to the problem with the tools that will actually increase the quality of the decisions that managers make!

Dr. John Sullivan is the Chief Talent Officer for Agilent Technologies and is on the Editorial Advisory Board of the IHRIM Journal. He is currently on leave as the head of HR at San Francisco State University. He can be reached at **JohnS@sfsu.edu**.

HRIS —
the Future:
A View from the Threshold
of the New Millennium

By Joel R. Lapointe

Where to begin? When first asked to gaze into my crystal ball and predict the future of human resource information systems (HRIS), I immediately recalled what my prep school biology teacher once said: "the history of the past predicts the evolution of the future." While he was clearly referring to species of plants and animals, his point seems applicable to the subject of this article. The history of HRIS (only about 30 years) is a reasonable predictor of what the future will be. So, let's look back quickly at the genetic make up of our HRIS industry, its DNA, if you will, to understand what the species may look like in the years to come.

Out of the primordial ooze of the computer age, arose the first elements of our HRIS life form. Some of us remember the MSA, McCormick & Dodge, InSci, and Genesys pioneers that first recognized the new characteristics of HR systems that distinguished them from their financial and accounting brethren. We observed three primary new characteristics:

1. The financial and accounting systems did not contain the capacity for needed human resources information such as education, skills, dependents, beneficiaries, performance, compensation, grade levels, development plans and training data. This was further evidenced in a closer examination of which human resources were actually represented in the new HRIS databases. Financially oriented payroll systems included human resources that were receiving a paycheck as "active," and if terminated, quickly "inactivated" these records (once the annual Form W-2 was issued). The new HR systems considered these same human resources as actively employed when they were receiving a paycheck, but some "employees," such as those on paid leave of absence, or those

87

receiving some severance pay continuation, were actually "inactive" from the HR perspective, while "active" from the financial/payroll perspective. The examples of these subtle, but significant differences were numerous in the early evidence, and have become more so as the species has evolved. HR systems now routinely contain information about human resources who are not employees at all — they just want to be — applicant or contractor examples come to mind.

2. The new HRIS retained significant personnel action history that was well beyond the quarter-to-date, year-to-date buckets of the financial systems. The primary evolutionary reason for this new "gene" was the requirement to track the employment process for compliance with the social legislation (U.S. Equal Employment Opportunity, et al) of the 1960s. History capacity and sophistication, particularly "point-in-time" date stamping, remain dominant characteristics today, some 30 years later.

While the computer age has been progressing at a previously unheard of pace, and HRIS implementations have followed the latest technologies, the full benefit and impact of HRIS deployment is yet to be realized.

3. The new HRIS approached reporting very differently. While the financial and accounting systems produced reports, they did so on structured, fixed processing periods (pay cycles or period-end calendars). HRIS reporting was done in ad hoc unscheduled ways, focused on problem and trend analysis, where an answer to one question often generated more questions.

These fundamental characteristics of more data, more history and more reporting remain dominant "genes" in even the basic members of the HRIS species as we enter the new century.

Recent evolutionary steps have added one additional dominant "gene" — more users. No longer are the HRIS users limited to HR administrative and functional experts. Now, every employee, and even many "wanna-be" (applicants) or "used-to-be" (retirees) employees are active users of the HRIS.

At the risk of overdoing the biology analogy, it would be fair to state that the current state of the HRIS life-form could be a four-legged creature, with ever-lengthening limbs, one for data, one for history, one for reporting and one for users! There is, however, an unusual and disturbing dichotomy between the evolution of the HRIS and the evolution of the computer age that spawned it. While the computer age has been progressing at a previously unheard of pace, and HRIS implementations have followed the latest technologies, the full benefit and impact of HRIS deployment is yet to be realized. From the beginning, the goal of HRIS has been to eliminate the administrivia of employee recordkeeping, and enable the strategic and impactful deployment of the human assets of each organization. At no time in the history of HRIS is this goal more important.

From this brief historical backdrop, it can be seen that HRIS has retained its fundamental characteristics, is continuing to grow, and has yet to reach its full potential. Having been a part of the HRIS industry from the beginning, that untapped potential and continuing evolution is what I see in my crystal ball for the future. My own assessment is that we have more than enough technology, and will likely have more than enough for some time to come. The challenge of the future of HRIS rests much more with its use and impact, than on keeping up with the next technological wave. We are just beginning to realize the potential that effective HRIS deployment can have on how our employees work and behave, and how our enterprises and institutions perform.

This potential can be described in terms of the HRIS best practices that are evidenced in various organizational profiles. These profiles, and associated characteristics, are divided into three types.

While most HRIS professionals aspire to be part of a Type I best practice organization, few have reached this lofty plateau.

1. Type I organizations exhibit high competency/capability in the strategic use of HRIS in support of well-articulated and aligned business goals that intersect all human resources disciplines.

2. Type II organizations exhibit effective competency/capability in the use of HRIS within some human resource disciplines, but have the need to broaden the impact both across the human resources functions and upward to the overall business objectives.

3. Type III organizations exhibit basic operational effectiveness, such that data accuracy is reliable to support fundamental reporting needs within the primary human resources disciplines.

With so many companies "recovering" from the massive ERP implementation projects that were prompted by the Y2K bug, it is not surprising that many organizations are only at the Type III level. Such organizations have completed the implementation of the major software components, usually consisting of human resources, payroll and basic benefits information. Data maintenance processes and procedures are in place, and users (often only in the HR/Payroll/Benefits departments) are trained and proficient. Best practice in these organizations is reflected by quality, accurate information, well disciplined processes (albeit, still paper-clogged), and periodic reporting of key information such as headcount, turnover, organizational demographics, and necessary compliance reports. It is not unusual for Type III organizations to have extended their HR software impact via outsourced 401(k) providers and automated voice-based self-service for benefits open enrollment.

It is important to note that these "type" profiles are not directly related to company size in terms of revenue or number of employees. Large companies may find themselves at the Type III level, just as smaller companies may very well exhibit Type I best practices.

Moving up the scale, Type II organizations are beyond operational effectiveness and often have implemented capability for broader functional support and a wider user community. Recruitment automation, which provides applicant tracking, requisition processing, and position management features, is frequently in place for these organizations. Compensation planning and budgeting capability is another high priority function that is technologically supported in the Type II organizations. More widely available access, both for data maintenance and reporting, is another best practice characteristic found in Type II companies. These companies often have employee and manager self-service initiatives underway to reduce the "administrivia" and move the HR function into its desired, more strategic and business-aligned role. Type II companies are also likely to have established intranet strategies which support the dissemination of a wide variety of human resources information, such as policy guides, organizational directories, job openings, training course catalogs, etc.

The human resources function has long struggled for its proper place at the boardroom table. Without this vital link, the intersection of business objectives and strategic planning with HR initiatives has often been missing.

The distinguishing best practice characteristics of Type I organizations are highly integrated and complete databases, broad self-service access by employees and managers, harnessed intranet and Internet connectivity, and tightly aligned linkage between the goals of the business and human resources activities. These organizations recognize the human resources function as being responsible for building and maintaining its "high performance workforce." HR owns the "employee productivity agenda", and can demonstrate the value proposition for each activity, associated data element and related business processes. For example, by using HR data to identify all employees that are connected to the sales role within the company, and linking sales and commission statistics to these employees, it has been possible to identify "best performers." This information is used to develop competency and skill characteristics, which form the basis for a sales performance knowledge base that can be deployed across the Internet around the world. The linkage between the human resources software, the best practices surrounding its use, and the improvement in sales performance is compelling. This model can be applied to many key roles within the organization.

The future of HRIS within any particular organization can therefore be defined by:

1. determining the best practice "profile" that describes the current state of HRIS usage,
2. aligning business and HRIS objectives to achieve higher levels of HRIS impact,
3. developing the pace and priority of HRIS improvements that support these objectives, and
4. adopting the emerging HRIS technologies that enable these improvements.

◼ Determining the current state

While most HRIS professionals aspire to be part of a Type I best practice organization, few have reached this lofty plateau. As a framework for some self-evaluation, consider the following "basics" that should be commonly available from even a Type III HRIS "information backbone."

Does the HRIS enable:

➤ THE EMPLOYMENT FUNCTION
- to shorten "time-to-hire?"
- to reduce recruitment costs?
- to determine best hire sources?
- to automate applicant communications and candidate scheduling?

➤ THE COMPENSATION FUNCTION
- to automate annual salary planning/budgeting?
- to determine market versus internal salary level competitiveness?
- to conduct cross-functional equity analysis, both for base compensation and pace of progression?

➤ THE BENEFITS FUNCTION
- to automate the annual enrollment process (via telephone and via the Web)?
- to provide consistent practice, plan and policy answers to employee inquiries?

➤ THE TRAINING AND DEVELOPMENT FUNCTION
- to match employee talent inventories to strategic business directions?

• to define optimum career paths for management development?

• to capture, maintain and leverage the organizational "knowledge assets"?

If so, this organization is a solid Type III, and the next level is within reach. If not, the basics still need some work.

■ Aligning business and HRIS objectives

The human resources function has long struggled for its proper place at the boardroom table. Without this vital link, the intersection of business objectives and strategic planning with HR initiatives has often been missing. The current booming economy, low unemployment, and Internet-speed business transformation provides a key opportunity for HR. Growing, successful organizations rely increasingly on the energy, talent, innovation and experience of its employees as the cornerstone of its competitive advantage. As suggested in the Type I profile discussed earlier, the central theme of this alignment is the focus on developing a "high performance workforce" and HR's key role in driving the employee productivity agenda.

The evolution of the HRIS "genes" must also follow this central theme.

➤ Is the data content fully matured?

➤ Will the history enable the identification of "best performer" career paths?

➤ How effective are the reporting and analysis "genes?"

➤ Will the many and diverse users find ready access and ease-of-use?

■ Developing pace and priority

This step represents a significant challenge because too often there is too much to be done within limited time, resource allocation and budget parameters. Compromise and priority setting are needed to develop and plan achievable projects. Recognizing the historic administrative reputation that has been the frequent burden of the HR function, meaningful priorities must be established to change that reputation and relieve that "baggage."

The future of HRIS must be driven by its use and impact on the business goals of the organization. Therefore, HR may (should) forego improvements that are not directly connected to these objectives. This can require a different, more externally focused priority model. For example: deploying a new Web-based benefits enrollment capability may need to be secondary to deploying a skills/knowledge base that improves the performance of the sales staff. Improving the delivery of benefits policy and practice information to employees may need to be secondary to "cloning" the best recruiters to shorten hiring cycles and streamline applicant candidacy.

■ *Adopting emerging HRIS technologies*

Understanding and harnessing the emerging HRIS technologies can be simplified into a single theme:

"Ubiquitous access to improve employee effectiveness and performance."

The HRIS and the larger enterprise resource planning (ERP) implementations focused on improved efficiency. Faster functions, less paper, fewer processing steps and re-engineered organizations resulted in "doing things right." The future of HRIS is about "doing the right things." While there are certainly opportunities to continue to improve efficiency, effectiveness has now become the primary goal. And, employee effectiveness, in particular, is being linked to organizational effectiveness, which results in improved organizational performance.

The major emerging technology trend that will drive the future impact of HRIS is known broadly as "enterprise information portals." In simple terms, this can be defined as:

> "...a personalized homepage that contains focused, relevant information, and provides transactions, knowledge and business metrics, that increase individual effectiveness and improve enterprise performance..."

This is an Internet-enabled technology concept that provides a solution to what has been described as the "infoglut" problem. Today's knowledge worker, tapped into both an internal intranet and the external Web, has too much information and not enough time. Enterprise information portals address several aspects of this growing information overload problem by:

➤ providing and organizing employee role-specific information,
➤ increasing efficiency by saving time accessing disparate information,
➤ increasing attention to focused metrics and role-specific results,
➤ providing end-to-end transactions and workflow, and

➤ providing "approved" merchant (i.e. external) content.

To more fully understand the enterprise information portal concept, let's look again at the Type I example described earlier.

> ... by using HR data to identify all employees that are connected to the sales role within the company, and linking sales and commission statistics to these employees, it has been possible to identify "best performers." This information is being used to develop competency and skill characteristics, which form the basis for a sales perform-ance knowledge base, that can be deployed across the Internet around the world.

This organization is embarked on the deployment of an enterprise informa-tion portal focused on the employees that work in a sales role. When sales staff access their desktops, Webtops, even "smart phones," the portal provides the information that is going to improve the performance of employees in that role, such as contact follow-up schedules, proposal samples, customer information, competitor positioning, sample presentations, product pricing and availability. The portal provides the window into and organizing framework for the myriad data that is available from the HR and related ERP software sources.

The objective is the "high performance workforce," and HR can play the piv-otal role in sponsoring and harnessing the emerging technologies to achieve that goal.

The HRIS life form has evolved over the past 30 years with four distinctive characteristics, which continue to grow:

➤ virtually unlimited capacity for data about employees (past, present and future),

➤ comprehensive history of employee and organizationall-centric events,

➤ sophisticated analytical and reporting features, and

➤ diverse users both inside and outside the workplace.

The impact of HRIS on employee effectiveness and, therefore, organizational performance, is just beginning to be realized.

The future of HRIS is bright, un-endangered and filled with potential.

Welcome to the 21st century.

Joel R. Lapointe is Senior Vice President of The Hunter Group, a Renaissance Worldwide Company, where he directs the management consulting resources. He serves as a contributing columnist for the IHRIM Journal and can be reached at **joel_lapointe@hunter-group.com**.

HR and the Workplace — What will it be like in the year 2010?
A Vision of the Future

By James E. Spoor

The uncertainties of Y2K are now relegated to history as a non-event and the business of business is moving forward into the first decade — the "double zero decade" — of a new millennium. The anxieties and dire predictions of the recent past regarding Y2K will soon be forgotten, only to be replaced, from time to time, by new fads and hot topics that will in their turn capture the attention, imagination and budgets of technologists, consultants and business leaders.

Throughout this new decade, organizations will face new strategic issues in a rapidly changing and uncertain world of business. Nimble organizations, those that will survive and grow, will act and behave like gazelles — intensely focused, hypersensitive to even the slightest change in their environment, alert to competitive or survival threats, able to change direction on a near instant basis, and fast moving in response to change.

For these nimble organizations, the "double zero decade" will produce fundamental changes in the ways organizations conduct their business, in the ways that people perform their roles, in the employment relationship, and the way results are produced. Only one thing is certain — there will be no return to former standards of "normality" for businesses or for the HR profession. It is clear that HR, and the use of technology within all aspects of what we have known as HR, will be at the very core of much of the change that will be occurring.

Visioning what the HR profession will look like 10 years from now and being able to predict the role and impact of technology on the people aspects of the workplace is no small task. The vagaries and uncertainties of the future are complicated by the fact that today we are in the vortex of multiple revolutions

95

— an accelerating technology revolution, the Internet revolution, a revolution in how and where people work, revolutionary changes in the HR function, a global competitive revolution and the e-business revolution. Last, but not least, with the heightened levels of frustration, anger and disenchantment that exist in society, there is the potential for other social changes that will have an impact on the workplace.

Revolutionary changes are occurring in the demographics of the workforce and in the expectations that both management and employees have of their employers in general, and of the HR function, in particular.

It is no wonder that many people in HR and in other leadership functions feel much like the victim of a hurricane felt when he exclaimed, "everything that was nailed down is blowing loose." Such is the future for HR and for all organizational areas that are directly involved with the management of the workforce.

The tornadic forces that are driving fundamental change in the workplace today are many and they are all accelerating. Collectively, people involved in any area of workforce management finds themselves in the vortex of at least 10 revolutions, transformations and challenges.

➤ Virtually all production oriented industries find themselves facing continuing, pervasive global competitive challenges which are driving corporations, teams, and individuals to think and act in new and different ways in order to survive.

➤ Revolutionary changes are occurring in the demographics of the workforce. The aging of the population, the passing of the Baby Boomer bubble, the increasing shift to technology-based employment, the increased percentage of dual income families, increased competition for professional level staff, are all impacting how companies operate.

➤ With desktop and handheld computing power doubling on an 18-month basis, technological change is making even recently implemented equipment, processes, and methodologies obsolete and competitively ineffective in increasingly shortened life cycles.

➤ As knowledge and information are being recognized as strategic resources, revolutionary changes are occurring in the way knowledge and data are collected, accessed, managed, manipulated, evaluated, disseminated, and transformed into useful strategic and tactical information.

➤ The quality, relevance, applicability, and accessibility of information from a variety of automated system sources — both internal and external — is becoming increasingly significant to organizational success as companies strive for competitive advantages. The ability to integrate data from multiple and often heterogeneous sources is essential.

➤ The impact of the Internet, whether it involves transactional e-business activities or the access to necessary decision support and planning information using a variety of "i" systems, is changing the way businesses think about the markets they address and the customers they serve.

➤ The above factors are driving revolutionary changes in the business processes of most organizations. How things get done is being redefined on a continuing basis as organizations struggle to remain nimble and responsive to environmental change.

➤ Revolutionary changes are occurring in the demographics of the workforce and in the expectations that both management and employees have of their employers in general, and of the HR function, in particular.

➤ Shortages of critical skills are forcing revolutionary changes in the employment relationship. As competition becomes more and more intense, organizations will become increasingly innovative in establishing compellingly, attractive "engagement relationships" that bear less and less resemblance to traditional employment relationships. Uniquely talented individuals will serve multiple employers, work as part of virtual teams, enjoy new levels of flexibility, and operate under an increased level of "free agency" conditions.

➤ With the redefinition of individuals' personal lifestyles and professional career alternatives, the gap between the haves and the have-nots will widen. This is going to create pressures that will challenge the fundamental underpinnings for our political and social structure.

■ What does this mean to the future of the HR and workforce management functions for the next decade?

What this means to the HR function is that, over the next decade, the future for workforce management will be defined by a diversity of internal and external factors, many of which have not been experienced before. The HR function as we know it today will no longer exist within many companies by the end of the decade. HR will have morphed itself and gone through a rapid evolutionary process. It will have been transformed into a substantially different creature than it is today. The variety of tasks and accountabilities that are currently considered to be under the HR umbrella will be modified and/or dispersed —

many to line managers. Many of the gatekeeper review, approval and control functions currently fulfilled by HR will have been reduced to business rules that serve as the guideposts for the automation of processes and decisions. Leaders will be allowed to make mistakes and will be increasingly accountable for the impact of those mistakes.

While the compensation and benefits functions of today's HR structure will continue to fulfill many of the same planning and cost management functions they fulfill today, a preponderance of the on-going and process-oriented aspects of staffing, training, and HR services will be returned to the control and responsibility of the line manager. The strategic issues of staffing, the implementation of new employment relationships to meet limited term and fluctuating needs, the definition of strategic development plans, and other truly strategic issues will be directed by a new function. In recognition of this emerging need, during the first half of the "double zero" decade, there will be increased acceptance of an emerging "Workforce Management" function.

This renaming of the function and realignment of the strategic and tactical responsibilities will reflect the fact that the demands of the next decade will require major changes in the scope, content, and role of what we know today as the HR itself. Just as Personnel, the predecessor of HR, eventually had to be renamed in order to overcome the stigma and poor image perceptions that were broadly associated with "Personnel" and the people in it, there is today a need to again change the name of the HR function in order to re-define the role and expectations.

> *Leaders will be allowed to make mistakes and will be increasingly accountable for the impact of those mistakes.*

Over the last 25 years, HR has established a role definition that is widely accepted and understood. While that definition has been reasonably effective in meeting the needs of the '80s and '90s, the "double zero" decade poses a whole new set of requirements. Once again, it is time to lift the box from around the function, re-define its roles and responsibilities, and give the new and evolved function a new identity. This new Workforce Management function will take a broader and more strategic view of the needs that exist. This new strategically focused function will integrate the wide range of activities, tasks, and functions that relate to the effective placement, utilization and management of people in the workplace.

The newly framed Workforce Management function will still be responsible for assuring that many of the traditional HR needs are met, but more importantly, it will be much more involved in the strategic business planning processes. It will have a leadership role in the proactive and innovative creation of new models for the hybrid workplace, and be responsible for the creation and implementation of new and innovative employment relationships. Key to this will be a significant and highly integrative role in the identification of future needs for strategically vital competencies and in putting together the plans to assure the availability of those competencies and talents. Skill and competency management will take on many of the characteristics of the "just-in- time" (JIT) methodologies that have been in place for years on the procurement side of many manufacturing businesses. As part of this, the traditional role of recruitment will be augmented to include talent management and utilization.

The scope of this new Workforce Management function will include areas and responsibilities that have traditionally been outside the normal control and responsibilities of the HR function. Currently available technology enables functions and areas such as payroll, timekeeping, industrial health, workers compensation, stock option administration, retirement and 401(k) administration, productivity assessment, and other areas to be integrated into the new Workforce Management function.

...Workforce Management function will still be responsible for assuring that many of the traditional HR needs are met, but more importantly, it will be much more involved in the strategic business planning processes.

But, new leadership skills, new and more business oriented ways of thinking, new business perspectives, and new levels of strategic contribution to the business goals are necessary, if lifting the box from around the existing definitions and constraints associated with the HR function is going to occur.

The new Workforce Management function will also play a lead role in the redefinition of the roles and responsibilities of teams and work groups that have specific deliverable goals and objectives. Competition for strategic talent will drive the implementation of new team centered practices that include drafting, trading, and free agency concepts similar to those found in professional athletics. The Workforce Staffing function will be responsible for the proactive scouting of talent — again similar to the athletic scouting activities. Teams will be increasingly incented based on successes achieved. The role of the leader in a team-oriented environment will be increasingly similar to that of the quarterback or captain of an athletic team.

It is clear that effectively addressing the full spectrum of challenges, implementing the necessary changes, and achieving the resulting economic success will require not only the full efforts of corporate leadership, but also an unprecedented level of adaptability, cooperation, and progressive change on the part of both organized labor and the governments of the developed countries.

Significant adjustments will be necessary on the part of legislative and regulatory activities to accommodate the needs of the new millennium.

■ The facilitating role of technology

Underlying and supporting the organizational and strategic dimensions of change is the fact that the availability of new technology will continue to make formerly impossible things possible. The rate of technological advancement will continue to accelerate. Faster, smaller, easier and cheaper will be the mantra for the technology deliverables. The size, format, and footprint of technology deliverables will move from departmental desktop devices operating under the full control of the user organization to a mixture of hand held, pocket-sized integrated devices and wireless linkages that provide needed accessibility on a real-time basis to centralized processing and data storage capabilities. Instant access to all needed knowledge and to essential meaningful data will be a keystone for the successful enterprise.

The rate of technological advancement will continue to accelerate. Faster, smaller, easier and cheaper will be the mantra for the technology deliverables.

Voice interactions with the new devices will be used as frequently as keystrokes. Connectivity will be universal, real-time and wireless on a global basis. Within these pocket size devices will be a fully integrated phone, pager, voice messaging, video conferencing, e-mail, contact manager, calendar/scheduler, word processor, spreadsheets, OLAP analytical tools, database access and online reports. All of this will be wrapped into a single five ounce device that fits in your purse, pocket, or hangs inconspicuously on your belt.

For the production force, sensors on each person's device will replace time keeping systems and provide touch-free labor costing and labor distribution. For billable people, time and task recording will be automatically handled with little intervention other than final review. Business rules, routings, and processes will be handled transparently and notifications regarding events and conditions will be generated and distributed without human intervention. Even GPS services will be there for those who are traveling.

On a personal level, the same pocket-size device that you use at work will also contain you payroll records, your benefits information. Your checkbook will also be on the same device and at the checkout counter it will use a highly secure infrared (IR) beam to interact with merchant devices to effectively re-place your credit cards. To provide you with the security you need, the device will sense your biometrics and recognize you as the only authorized user. It will not work in the hands of another person. The keyboard and display for the device will fold neatly into a final footprint no larger than today's digital phone.

... think tank studies already predict that by the mid-point in the "double zero" decade, over 50 percent of the jobs in North America will be either in the technology industries or in high technology utilization roles.

Within corporations, this enhanced use of technology and full access to real-time information and decision support capabilities will create the information-intense, no excuses, environment as far as decision-makers and leaders are con-cerned. But, that still leaves the question of what will the new worker be like and what will they be doing?

■ The new workforce

North America will have completed its transition to a predominantly infor-mation and services economy. As agricultural innovations and increased use of technology continue to occur, a declining percentage of the population will be engaged in agriculture and food production. As global competitive forces and high North American pay and benefits levels continue to drive unskilled jobs to developing countries, a declining percentage of the population will be involved in production and hourly labor roles. Continuing technology and communica-tions advances will put clerical and administrative roles under constant scrutiny, challenge and reduction. Entertainment and hospitality services will be the last hope for those with limited skills. Even the military will have achieved reduced staffing levels and, through continued exploitation of technology, will be able to provide an improved total capability to deal with challenges to security and peace. As career politicians, bureaucrats, and lawyers continue to strive to pro-tect the status quo and constrain even positive change and progress, govern-ment will be the last bastion for "old ways of doing things" and low productivity.

As for the private sector, think tank studies already predict that by the mid-point in the "double zero" decade, over 50 percent of the jobs in North America will be either in the technology industries or in high technology utilization roles. Other studies indicate that substantial growth in the numbers of fully flexible or boundary-less workers will occur. A wide variety of pressures will drive these shifts. In many respects, individuals with "star level" key strategic and technological skills and competencies will become "free agents" and "fix it" contractors to organizations. They will be brought in to deliver their unique expertise when and where limited term efforts are required.

The shrinking core group of key professional and leadership employees in organizations will still be treated as "regular full time" employees, but even they will enjoy significant increases in when and where they actually do their work. External pressures including dependent care needs, traffic congestion, urban problems, commuting costs and frustrations, limited office space, and other environment related issues will cause organizations to revisit and expand the old concepts of flextime and variable workplaces. Subject to having a requirement for a very limited amount of time — several hours each week or each month — in the primary office or workplace for face to face interaction and to maintain and preserve personal relationships, work time for many will be broadened to encompass extensive choice within a 24X7 framework and choice of workplace venue. Personal preferences will be the driving motivator and technology will make it possible and highly productive.

The new generation of technology-focused workers will increasingly select their employers based on the culture of the organization as much as on the traditional considerations.

■ The demographics of the new workforce

The Baby Boomers will be at or approaching retirement. The bubble that they currently represent in the workforce population will have disappeared. The new bubble that they will represent is as part of the aging, non-working population. Fewer and fewer productive workers will be supporting a larger and larger population of retired individuals.

The new era of individuals, born and raised without having experienced massive economic hardships or without having been through a period of threats to the security and survival of the democratic society, will now be responsible for providing leadership and innovation to the business setting. Their views regarding personal responsibility and accountability will increasingly confront traditional standards. The cultural shift in the workforce will be significant. This will be a major challenge to the role of the new Workforce Management function.

As organizations develop, modify, and institutionalize their respective corporate cultures and values, diversity will take on a new meaning. With the depersonalization of society and the erosion of other centers of social contact outside of the workplace, the workplace and the personal contacts established in the workplace become more and more a social focus for employees. With this being the case, the new generation of technology focused workers will increasingly select their employers based on the culture of the organization as much as on the traditional considerations. The workplace and the employer relationship will be meeting new needs and experiencing new challenges.

■ Summary

Back to the earlier quote of the person caught in the hurricane — "everything that was nailed down is blowing loose." We are facing tremendous tornadic influences on the way we live and work. As we are entering the "double zero" decade, these tornadic influences are driving us into a period of potentially enormous change. Technology is, in many cases, driving the change. In other cases, it is facilitating and enabling the change. As we look to the future, it is clear that there are major changes in store for the way our organizations operate and, in particular, for the function we currently know as HR. Those who are able to see the opportunity and the needs of the new Workforce Management function — and learn to rapidly exploit the use of technology in meeting those needs — will be highly successful.

Jim Spoor is Founder, President and CEO of Spectrum Human Resource Systems Corporation and on the Board of Directors of IHRIM. He serves on the Editorial Advisory Board of the IHRIM Journal and can be reached at **jspoor@spectrumhr.com**.

Action Items for the HR Executive:
A "To Do" List in the First Decade of the New Millennium

By Marc S. Miller

The major issues and/or action items facing HR executives as the new millennium begins can be stated as a seven point "To Do" List:

1. RECRUIT AND RETAIN YOUR "KNOWLEDGE WORKERS"
2. LEVERAGE YOUR COSTLY ERP IMPLEMENTATION IN ORDER TO PROVIDE A POSSIBLE REVENUE STREAM (BEYOND COST SAVINGS)
3. OBTAIN A "TOTAL COMPENSATION" QUANTIFICATION AND USE IT IN A RETAINMENT STRATEGY
4. ALIGN THE HR FUNCTION WITH OVERALL CORPORATE BUSINESS STRATEGIES
5. IMPLEMENT BUSINESS PROCESS IMPROVEMENTS THAT INCORPORATE EMPLOYEE AND MANAGER SELF-SERVICE SUPPORTED BY THE ESTABLISHMENT OF "CENTERS OF EXCELLENCE" AND "SHARED SERVICES CENTERS"
6. OUTSOURCE WHAT IS *NOT* IN HR'S CORE COMPETENCIES
7. SEEK A REVENUE STREAM FOR HR THROUGH PARTNERSHIPS WITH CONTENT PROVIDERS ON E-COMMERCE OFFERINGS TO YOUR EMPLOYEE POPULATION

■ Recruit and retain your "Knowledge Workers."

A recent issue of *Business Week* magazine (December 6, 1999) had as its cover story, "The Wild New Workforce — What it takes to hire and keep the modern worker." This lead story described how companies must "play by new rules" in their dealings with their current employees and what they need to offer to recruit and retain top talent. The article stated that "just as the New Economy is dismantling the old rules of commerce, the new workforce is shredding the contracts between employers and employees. Employers are giving up rigid wage scales in favor of flexible compensation. They are learning to live with high turnover and abolishing seniority based pay — we are moving towards person based-pay." Employees who remain loyal to a company and stick around are penalized. "After all, if the woman in the next cubicle can jump to another company for a 20% raise, a signing bonus, and stock options, why should she wait around for that 4% merit hike?"

> *More than half of all organizations, with enterprise resource planning (ERP) systems in place, plan to integrate those systems with existing or planned e-commerce systems.*

It is clear that these new "rules" and practices are changing the workforce employee dynamic. The pressure is squarely on the HR function for providing leadership, and best practices enabling the organization to keep its talented workers ("knowledge workers") at a minimum, and at the same time position itself to compete with its competitors for new talent. This clearly is a most critical issue facing HR executives in this first decade of the new millennium. Additionally, keep in mind that:

➤ Knowledge Workers are those employees that an organization values most; they offer the organization desirable competencies, and they are not easily replaced.

➤ The workforce is the one component that competitors cannot easily duplicate quickly.

➤ All employees, and especially Knowledge Workers, must be aware of their *total compensation* if the organization hopes to retain its most valuable human resources.

■ *Leverage your costly ERP implementation in order to provide a possible revenue stream beyond cost savings.*

➤ More than half of all organizations, with enterprise resource planning (ERP) systems in place, plan to integrate those systems with existing or planned e-commerce systems. This unique opportunity will allow the HR function to become a generator of revenue for the organization it supports by allowing external product and service providers fee-based access to a population of employees.

■ *Obtain a "Total Compensation" quantification and use it in a retainment strategy.*

➤ "Employers are giving up rigid wage scales in favor of flexible compensation. They are learning to live with high turnover and abolishing seniority-based pay" — "The Wild New Workforce," *Business Week*, December 6, 1999.
➤ ERP systems must be able to produce an accurate picture of total compensation for each of the organization's employees.

■ *Align the HR function with overall corporate business strategies.*

➤ The traditional HR function has often been perceived by the organization it supports as both paternalistic and obsessed with legal compliance; the unfortunate result has been an unhealthy relationship between HR and the rest of the organization.
➤ The new HR must change and become the enabling force that helps the organization realize its business goals and objectives.
➤ HR must be proactive in its ability to provide the board of directors of the organization the information (not data) they need to strategically guide the organization.

■ *Implement business process improvements that incorporate employee and manager self-service, supported by the establishment of "Centers of Excellence" (COE) or "Shared Service Centers."*

➤ Critical to the success of HR self-service is the "back office" infrastructure needed to support an employee or manager request for information or transaction completion.

➤ Many organizations have pursued the development a Shared Services Center, sometimes called a Center of Excellence or simply a Call Center.

➤ The Shared Service function, COE, or Call Center can be staffed internally or outsourced, depending on such factors as staff experience, economics and culture of the organization.

Examples of Opportunities for Cost Savings:

➤ *Information Week* magazine provides the statistics that the cost of routine HR transactions typically falls from as much as US$17 to just US$2.40 when self-service technology is employed.

> *When an existing HR function does not offer those competencies required to support the organizational mission, outsourcing may be the most cost-effective and efficient solution.*

➤ Following the UK merger of Glaxo and Wellcome, the executives found that "trying to find an employee and figure out who they reported to was impossible." Part of the solution was moving to self-service for employees. The result was a decrease in cost of transactions by 50% and a shift in the nature of the total work from being 60% transactional to only 10% transactional.

➤ The self-service solution introduced by a major U.S. oil company with 9,000 employees to handle the distribution of benefits statements and electronic pay stubs saved US$370k in the first year alone, due to reduced paperwork, postage and staff time.

➤ Sony significantly reduced its headcount (12%) and expects future cost savings of 25-30%. In addition, service levels and quality/timeliness of information have improved, average cycle time of existing HR processes has been reduced by 28%, and HR services are more aligned with the overall business strategy.

➤ Ford estimates its global HRMS will save an estimated >US$5 million/year following the full implementation (project is projected to be completed 09/15/2001).

Current status of the project:
- ➤ HR Service Center with one million + calls — 92% customer satisfaction
- ➤ HR Web site with two million + user transactions in the first two months — 96% customer satisfaction
- ➤ New tiered-service delivery model
- ➤ HR transactions successfully from Line HR to Shared Services and Self-Service.
- ➤ Mitsubishi — Reduced cost per call (to HR) from US$48 to US$3.

■ Outsource what is NOT in HR's core competencies.

➤ Many organizations have identified outsourcing as a strategy to reduce costs.

➤ Executives and boards of directors have narrowed their respective focus to increasing market share and creating products and services to meet customer demand; the HR function has been called on more than ever to be the enabling force that helps the organization reach its goals and objectives.

➤ Each HR executive's team offers the organization a given set of competencies. When an existing HR function does not offer those competencies required to support the organizational mission, outsourcing may be the most cost-effective and efficient solution.

■ Seek a revenue stream for HR through partnerships with content providers on e-commerce offerings to your employee population.

➤ Capitalize on the concept of "Employee-Facing Portals." Also known as an "employee dashboard" or "employee Web-top," a portal serves as a single front-end point of entry for employees accessing a corporate or HR intranet. This concept goes well beyond the typical static home page employed by most HR or corporate organizations, because the portal is customized for the individual employee who uses it. Additionally, it provides visible evidence of the company's support of a "Work/Personal Life Balance" approach that is critical in retaining the knowledge worker.

➤ Taking the portal concept one step forward and assuming HR is the rightful owner of the corporation's employee facing Internet functions, the potential for revenue generation becomes clear. External providers of Web-based products and services are given exclusive access to a population of employees, and a small transaction fee is charged in return for that privilege. Employees can be incented to do their online shopping during non-business hours, while receiving a discount from the provider of the product or service they purchase.

➤ Product or service providers such as BarnesandNoble.com, Amazon.com, and Rock Financials have already entered into such agreements with corporations. For example, a $2.00 fee paid to HR for every mortgage or refinance sold to the employee population has the potential to create a significant amount of revenue. The cost of implementation can be cost-justified using the potential revenue generated, eventually leading to a true positive cash flow for the HR function. Merrill Lynch has already recognized this opportunity and is moving to implement practices that will realize a steady revenue stream directly to the corporate HR function.

➤ The concept of an HR revenue stream, quantifiable and visible to senior management, can make almost anything possible if leveraged properly.

Marc S. Miller is the Managing Director/MCS/HRM/Energy for PricewaterhouseCoopers LLP. He is founder and formerly president of Marc S. Miller Associates. He can be reached at **marc.s.miller@ us.pwcglobal.com**.

HRIM Directions
as We Enter
the 21st Century

By Mike Method

Do you have a modern HRIS in place? Does it cover all of your employees? Is the data accurate, timely, and complete? Have you minimized the massive administrative tasks surrounding benefits enrollment and personal information management by offering employee self-service? Have you provided managers with meaningful self-service applications for use against their direct reports? Is your HRIS nicely coordinated or integrated with your timekeeping and payroll operations? Do you provide usable and effective reporting tools, along with appropriate access to them? If so, congratulations! You have the core pieces necessary to support the basic HRIS functions, and you are well positioned to move your HRIS into the 21st century.

As you read the last sentence, you might have been thinking, "Wait just a minute! We have spent enormous effort and expense to develop a great system already. I've got what I need." My premise is that you're now ready to begin to truly support not only the HR function, but also the rest of your organization's management and employees. The directions in the next few years will be towards those broader objectives.

As we enter the 21st century, HR must expand its understanding of information, what is possible and, most importantly, what is needed. We now have the experience and the computer power to expand the depth, breadth, reach, and integration of our systems into the entire fabric of our organizations and processes. We need to establish a more holistic, organic approach to the opportunities. HR information management needs to support management, not just HR!

When we survey the expo floor, attend educational sessions at IHRIM or other conferences and read HR or technical publications, we get an outstanding picture of current technologies and vendor applications. They reflect processes and capabilities that are available now.

Moving beyond the HRIS core, we have four key directions:

1. to extend the scope and reach of our applications,

2. to expand the population covered by its capabilities,

3. to embed data from HR applications in the other functions of the business, and

4. to improve management analysis of the workforce.

Let's take a look at each of these.

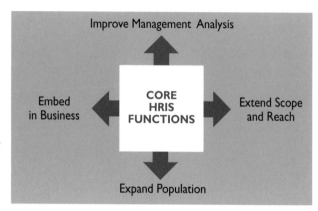

■ *Extending the Scope and Reach*

The dimensions of HRIM opportunities certainly include core HRIM functions, with employee personal data, compensation, benefits and related records. Those are joined by (or tightly integrated with) timekeeping, payroll, performance measurement, management development, expatriate and other employee specific record data. More aggressive and progressive installations will be using active position management to complete the core picture. Finally, there should be a robust capability for everyone in HR to have access to adequate reporting tools.

The last 40 years of progress for HR information has been driven by computer technology, by process changes and by organizational concepts. Those have certainly been interrelated. In the last decade, they have permitted us to get beyond the basics and move aggressively toward extending the capabilities of the core applications and adding new applications. Examples include applicant tracking, performance measurement, management development, competency modeling, compensation modeling, training administration and employee attitude surveys. We have dramatically expanded who could use the systems, how quickly the tasks could be done, how readily we could integrate applications or move the data between systems, and how many things we could do.

With limited exceptions, developments have supported the traditional view of "personnel." We now call it "HR" but, for most organizations, the focus has continued to be on basic personnel records for the typical salaried and hourly employee populations. The focus has been from an HR perspective, despite catch phrases about "supporting the business."

The capabilities have been made more robust, but in far too many cases, they have not been adequately supported with effective processes or system edits to ensure the completeness and quality of the information they purport to provide. Both core and extended applications need to build processes and technology that enable — and require — accurate and adequate data, gathering the information correctly the first time with minimum effort and maximum effectiveness. Designing system or administrative processes that require "audit" reports to detect problems or are dependent on secondary or follow-up efforts to complete the information is wasted effort, in both time and resources. Equally important, each additional and separate effort that is required adds to the problem by creating more points where the process can fail. Gather the correct information — in the right format — the first time — from the right source.

■ Expanding the Population

Next, HR organizations and management will recognize that they need to expand the population because they are really in the "people" business. They need to account for and support several people-populations that are not direct employees, including agency and contract employees, consultants, on-site outsourced services, etc. There are several reasons for this. As organizations reduce their internal headcount, they are increasingly relying on contingent workforces to accomplish tasks — workforces that need to be tracked and analyzed for skills, budget, facility and other purposes. Various administrative and government processes, which are associated most frequently with HR, effectively force everyone to be dealt with, for example U.S. OSHA and security badges. From the perspective of the typical manager or employee, there is an expectation that common services, such as telephones and computer facilities, will have common information and processes for the populations they serve.

Are there risks and complexities to this? Of course, there are. But, gathering differing information for varying populations is nothing new, difficult or extraordinary. We typically record certain different information for hourly and salaried employees, for managers or executives, for sales force and more. Keeping records discreet and gathering critical information about your contingent workforce does not need to compromise any legal distinctions for "employees" or add any significant burden to processes. Based on experience, I expect that most organizations would see a net reduction in the effort spent to track, report and analyze this very real and critical population.

■ Embedding HR in the Business Processes

Third, HR needs to be embedded in the business processes. We will see more organizations expecting HR to support the business from their operating and staff perspectives, not simply from a parochial HR posture.

Today, HR may be congratulating itself for supporting the business because it is more aggressively and intelligently handling the recruiting, performance evaluation, training, and leadership development efforts, frequently by using the Web and other resources to make the tasks easier, more robust and directly available to the management or employee. But, it has not extended its resources and information to serve the tasks which others need to do every day. The effort here is not just shifting workload but a need to establish a "buy-in" from others.

What has not been recognized is the critical support that other functions need. The finance/accounting function has needs for organization, budget, travel expense administration, and other activity, which require either individual or summary information about the workforce and the organization. Likewise, the purchasing function needs to constantly know the organization's incumbents and reporting relationships, so that it can deal with levels of authority and route processes accurately. The systems function needs timely and accurate information on active/inactive employees, transfers, management levels, reporting relationships, and other factors that impact the deployment of resources and myriad security concerns. And, line management needs support for everything from mundane telephone emergency contact lists to organization directories to workforce scheduling. The opportunities continue with the potential of employee information for your marketing, public relations, stockholder records, product development/testing or other organizations.

. . . there needs to be a dramatic improvement in the availability, understanding, and use of analytical tools that truly support management analysis of the workforce.

It is also true that HR needs information from the other functions. For example, HR may already be obtaining some payroll data, e.g., overtime hours and dollars paid, but are you able to gather information about other aspects of their employment? If you are dealing with position management, compensation management or organizational development, much of this data could be very interesting. Are you aware of the dollars, hours, and other expenses incurred by your contingent workforce? If you have remote or telecommuting employees, do you have good measurement of their impact?

■ *Improving Management Analysis*

Fourth, there needs to be a dramatic improvement in the availability, understanding, and use of analytical tools that truly support management analysis of the workforce.

In the next few years, this will become much more than basic reporting. It will mean significant advances in your ability to provide predictive analysis and data mining for your internal workforce. If you can gather and correlate a wide variety of the employee data discussed above; employee opinion data, systems usage and budget data, external data from census, U.S. Bureau of Labor Statistics, or other sources, then you can develop a much more robust picture of how your workforce is evolving, the gaps which need to be filled, the pressure points which need to be addressed, and the risk factors to achieving your corporate objectives. Ultimately, this will support much more confident and effective management decisions.

Most organizations at present do even basic reporting and workforce analysis poorly, in large part by assuming that an educated workforce equipped with adequate reporting tools will do it well. This assumption is woefully mistaken. In order to be effective, the analyst certainly must know how to use the reporting tools but, far more importantly, he or she must know and understand all of the available data, its reliability, the populations to which it applies, its completeness and its implications. This is not at all self-evident. And, having understood and obtained analytical data, the analyst must be able to present the findings meaningfully, so that the results have maximum impact. The bottom line is that capturing all of that data does no good unless you can effectively use it.

There certainly are a number of companies and consultants who are proficient at assembling disparate data for analytical purposes, but it doesn't reach everyone. A very few companies or government organizations have established sufficient expertise to actively achieve any serious predictive capabilities.

Much more attention and effort needs to be focused on teaching employees to understand the information that is available to them. Part of this will include developing and using effective data dictionaries. And, part of it will include educating the employees so they understand how all that data is actually organized, and then how to make the most effective use of the tools to achieve the reporting objective.

The software tools are improving and that will make a difference. Spreadsheet and presentation graphics software are drawing back the curtain on both what can be expected and what is possible. Some of the data warehouse tools are beginning to provide part of the technical capability. Sophisticated templates and application software will be developed which simplify or amplify the employee capabilities.

Ultimately, however, there is an expertise and art to achieving this next level of sophistication. Technical expertise will always remain critically dependent on the quality, completeness and other factors discussed above.

As we move into the new millennium, I expect that more and more attention will be paid to this issue. Every organization needs to devise effective standards for analysis and encourage effective presentation skills.

■ Conclusion

Finally, the reader should note that I have used few references to the technical tools.

Technology will continue to improve or be invented. We've developed through the eras of mainframes, minicomputers, PCs, and client/server systems. Data storage capacities have gone through the roof. We've seen fax forms, scanning, bar coding, and document management systems, along with kiosks, voice response systems and smart cards. And, today we are dealing with the explosion of Web and wireless technologies. All of these will continue to be valuable and used (yes, even mainframes!), and new technologies are right around the corner.

Ultimately, however, the concepts presented here are organic to the future of the HR function and information management: extending the scope and reach of our applications, expanding the population, embedding data from HR applications in other functions and improving management analysis of the workforce.

Mike Method is Principal, Methods Unlimited, and a member of the IHRIM Board of Directors. With more than 30 years experience, Method was formerly Global HRIS Manager at Ford Motor Company. He can be reached at **MJMethod@aol.com**.

IT-enabled HR

By Dave Russo

The merging of human resources functions and technology in recent years has enabled great gains in process automation and efficiency within the enterprise. Companies now must go beyond mere process automation and use technology to enable the strategic value of the HR function in a manner that emphasizes the importance, not only of employee data, but of employees.

Today, more than half of U.S. companies now conduct human resources transactions over the Web according to the Watson Wyatt consulting firm. And, this number continues to rapidly increase. Automating tasks such as payroll processing and benefits administration is freeing HR practitioners from paperwork and repetitive tasks. The tangible benefits of the technology are that employees are able to exploit their own data, reviewing, confirming and changing information relevant to their personal history or job function as well as taking ownership of data sources that were previously interdependent, but unconnected. The automation of these functions also provides the tangible benefit of offering employees a direct communication line to the HR function that may not have existed before the technology.

"Technology and human resources now are inseparable," says Jenni Lehman, research director for administrative applications strategies at the GartnerGroup, a Stamford, Connecticut-based market analysis firm in a recent issue of *Workforce*. Today, understanding how to use systems and software to solve problems and manage work is essential. HR is becoming a key differentiator for highly successful organizations. That is a trend that is going to continue to accelerate."

■ From Back Room to Boardroom

The key differentiator for highly successful organizations in the coming years will not be whether or not they are using technology, but rather, how are they using technology. Web-enabling the provision of statistical data on headcount or workforce diversity, for instance, may better serve HR functions in the exchange of information with their company's accounting, payroll and legal departments and the like. But, for the HR function to reach its potential as a strategic asset for the company, it must use technology to surface data to drive decision-making that impacts the organization's bottom line.

Exploiting data through technology can provide the insight a corporation needs to enact forward thinking strategies for attracting and retaining the knowledge worker that will proliferate in the next millennium.

Data is not strategic. However, the proper use of technology can turn that raw data into meaningful strategic information that can be used to aid decision-making. The demographics of a workforce are merely the "what." The information that can be gleaned from that data can provide the "what if" and create direct bottom line impact.

Turning raw data into useful information is the real value technology brings to the human resources function by enabling HR practitioners to demonstrate in numbers and conversely, in dollars, how decisions that affect employees affect the bottom line. By integrating data, much of which likely exists within the enterprise, such as employee turnover or job satisfaction, analyzing, reporting and weighting the information against other factors or forecasting data, business decisions on critical matters ranging from workforce expansion to cost cutting can be made strategically. In doing so, technologies like data warehousing and decision support software will move the HR function from the back room to the boardroom.

■ New Workplaces Demand New Approaches

The driving force behind an organization's move toward technology need not be to plan for the future. The changing workforce of today demands faster, smarter approaches to attracting and retaining talent. For instance, in IT industries the demand for specialized skills and know-how is expected to continue to outstrip supply during the next five to 10 years, according to Dianne Tunick Morello in the June 1999 issue of the IHRIM *Journal*. IT employers are already struggling with the realities of how a tremendous demand for talent, coupled with a shortage of skilled employees, has created a competitive marketplace and forced employers to rethink many of their HR strategies. Exploiting data through technology can provide the insight a corporation needs to enact forward thinking strategies for attracting and retaining the knowledge worker that will proliferate in the next millennium.

The IT sector is not alone in terms of new challenges for HR. During the next ten years, the labor force will continue to grow — and grow more diverse. More women will enter the workforce and the number of Hispanics and Asians will rise rapidly. The aging of the Baby Boomer generation will result in a rise in the median age of the labor force to record levels according to the U.S. Department of Labor, *Monthly Labor Review*, November 1999. But, the bigger news may lie in the simple fact that organizations are struggling to maintain their competitive advantage as fewer and fewer qualified candidates entering the job market.

In the old way of doing business, the primary role of HR would be to record these changes and monitor workforce diversity, demographics and the rest in an incidental manner. Through the use of technology, HR practitioners can predict and possibly influence change. By using data to forecast the changing dynamics of their workforce and affect decision-making to meet the needs of both employees and employer, technology will enable HR to take its role as a strategic partner in the enterprise.

Decision-support reporting tools are only as effective as the data within them and the people behind them. Technology alone will not cure the ills of an organization whose human resources philosophies are inherently misguided. A technology plan is not what is needed by most businesses to be successful in the next millennium. A human resources plan, which technology can enable, is the foundation for success within the enterprise.

■ New Skills for "Not New" Employees

Moore's Law says that microprocessors double in speed and their prices are cut in half every two years. HR practitioners need to be aware of how the rapid expansion of technology affects the people who use those microprocessors. Some estimate that employees in a technology field should expect to see 20 percent of their skills become obsolete every 12 to 18 months.

Successful businesses know the importance of retaining employees in a climate where competition for qualified people is fierce and employee turnover hovers in the teens. And more and more, retraining employees is going to be a key component in retaining employees.

As the need of the enterprise grows to attract and retain flexible, knowledge workers who may have an area of expertise, but are not specialists in the traditional sense, so too will HR have to adapt to this changing landscape. HR will move away from silos of compensation and benefits and demand for practitioners that can embrace technology while keeping a clear understanding of HR business rules. The function needs to be technology and business-centered in order to play a significant role in the construction of organization's strategic planning.

> *... technology used properly enables employers to get a better, more complete understanding of the true value of HR and "human assets" to the enterprise.*

The need for knowledge and training must also go beyond the frontline worker and reach all levels of the organization. HR has to become a champion of developing leadership and management skills. While we have learned that employee loyalty is a scarce commodity, we have also learned that loyalty does not always rest where we have traditionally expected to find it. The loyalty of employees to the enterprise is limited. Leadership skills can create relationships between individuals that go beyond the enterprise.

People's skills and their ability to meet new challenges must continually change and expand along with business needs. Ultimately, it's the people behind the technology — not the technology itself — that will make the real difference in any company's success.

■ *Maintaining the Human Element*

The key asset any employee brings to a company today is knowledge. Conversely, when an employee leaves a company, that knowledge also walks out the door. Attracting and retaining employees becomes even more critical in the face of these new realities. While the paths of HR and IT must converge in order to meet the new demands of the workplace, it is in this arena that the two paths must also diverge.

Perhaps the greatest inherent risk with the increased use of technology in the HR arena is that the "human" aspect of human resources will be lost. It is paramount for any organization to maintain the understanding that they are not dealing merely with "data" or "assets," but with people. To do that, these new tools have to be personalized to the level of the Windows interface. They need to be facile and common sense for HR people so they can surface, mix and match data to meet the ever changing landscape of expectations within the enterprise of the human side of business.

Just a few years ago, one of the great hurdles between HR and the use of technology was that the automation of functions would cost HR practitioners their jobs. We now know that the reality is that the use of technology has freed HR practitioners from repetitive tasks and allowed them to use their time to think strategically.

Likewise, steps must be taken to ensure that the use of technology does not lead to employees being treated simply as numbers on a spreadsheet, but rather, that technology used properly enables employers to get a better, more complete understanding of the true value of HR and "human assets" to the enterprise.

■ Competitive Advantage

Using technology to exploit the strategic value of the human resources function has become a source of competitive advantage for highly successful organizations in today's business environment. A human resources plan that uses the power of decision-support technology to help strategic planning by exploiting information is becoming the foundation of organizational success. However, technology implemented without regard to human capital is a grave mistake. An organization whether today, tomorrow or well into the future, will only go as far as the people they attract and retain will take them. Technology is the foundation for success, but people are, and will continue to be, the bricks to competitive advantage.

Dave Russo is the Executive Vice President of Human Resources for Buildnet, a leading provider of building management software based in Research Triangle Park, North Carolina. He is formerly the Vice President of Human Resources for SAS Institute, Inc. He can be reached at **drusso@buildnet.com**.

Component-Based Technology for the Next Decade

By John Macy

As we look towards the next decade and predict what is going to be the next wave of technology that will influence the human resource (HR) profession, I believe component-based technology (CBT) will almost certainly lead the way. I am not basing this prediction on the natural evolution of current technology or inside knowledge of the future release of the current major human resource information system (HRIS) vendors; technology, no matter how elegant, will not succeed unless it achieves business acceptance. I base this on some fairly confident assumptions relating to a new technology trend far more aligned to the business requirements of the 21st century and the success of which will be guaranteed by two very predictable characteristics of human behavior — personal ambition and personal financial gain.

From a personal ambition perspective, I don't believe individuals working in HR are seriously motivated at a departmental or division level. We may all agree that HR should have a place in the boardroom and should be elevated in the eyes of the organization, but the reality is that individuals want to advance their personal career by looking good and acting more professionally (rather than looking good as a department). The technology tools to allow them to be more professional are becoming available, and enabled through CBT. In the 1980s, being able to use spreadsheet software made a finance person look far more professional than their peers, who could only use a calculator. As we go into the next century, the ability to apply component software to support the HR business specialty will make the HR person more professional than their peer group who rely on outdated inflexible HRIS systems or manual processes.

As for financial gain, fierce competition and product differentiation has always been a feature of the HR software business. As we have seen with recent trends towards products providing features such as workflow, Web enablement, enterprise resource planning (ERP) solutions, and more recently portals, there is a definite financial advantage in getting to the market first. So it will be with CBT. At present, the main beneficiaries of CBT are the application integration specialists who are meticulously joining up front-end enterprise applications to back-end legacy systems with the precision of a micro surgeon rejoining a severed limb. The economics of software delivery are about to change. A much simpler and more open "plug in" approach will be a feature of the new CBT revolution. The difference with the CBT revolution is that everyone who ever wrote a line of code will be able to join in the financial spoils. The CBT revolution will be driven by new market forces and everyone from current HRIS vendors to development teams based in the foothills of the Himalayas will want to be part of the new wave of technology.

A component is a self-contained entity that can be compiled and sold on its own. It is not a complete HRIS, but multiple components can be plugged into a framework to form an HR "system."

For those who are unfamiliar with component based technology concepts, a component is a module, representing an HR business function (such as performance management) that sits behind the items on the HR menu. When an item is chosen, it will invoke an application, or a report, or a portal of some sort. In technical terms, a component is a "large-grained business object." A component is a self-contained entity that can be compiled and sold on its own. It is not a complete HRIS, but multiple components can be plugged into a framework to form an HR "system."

Software developers have actually been using components for some time as the micro building blocks of an application, such as icons, radio buttons, pulldown windows, etc. The CBT development technique has been used widely in building utility software products for many years. For example, spreadsheets use component development techniques.

There are different kinds of component "families" needed to build a human resource application. Some components perform basic transactional updating of an HR database, other components retrieve data from the HR database and present information to users in the form of reports, and portal components assist HR business processes by providing a Web-based interface to access, display and update information.

Underpinning the architecture of CBT is a framework and a database. The framework provides the core system functions, such as menus, audit, security, database access control and the component plug in points. The database has a common table structure and naming convention for the data elements used by all components accessing a human resource database.

The following may help to explain how each type of component fits into the overall CBT human resource "system" architecture:

➤ THE DATABASE COMPONENT

This permanent layer of the component architecture is the first purchase made. It does not change when plug-in components change or need to be upgraded. The table and file structures are defined by a Standard (expected to become available soon) and, if it becomes necessary to add fields or tables at a later stage, the database management system has the capability of doing that.

➤ FRAMEWORK COMPONENT

This component represents the "core" of the component architecture. It contains the structure for the software repository or the library map of where components are stored. It would usually be delivered with the start-up menu screens and the base component products such as positions and organisation. After the database, this is the second component purchased.

➤ TRANSACTIONAL COMPONENTS

These components are the actual transactions that support HR business functions. They update the database and contain the business rules that perform functions, validate the data and protect the integrity of the database.

➤ REPORT COMPONENTS

Report components are pre-written reports that represent a company's information needs from the database. The CBT Standard permits reports that are compliant to be on-sold or reused after a conversion to another component or set of components (amounting to the equivalent of a new HRIS). The characteristics of report components are that they use the common table and field name standards, and they use a reporting product that allow them to be packaged and plugged-in.

Reports do not have to be limited to standard data extractions listing employees and totals. They can be data feeds to Web browsers, extracts for export to spreadsheets, etc.

➤ PORTAL COMPONENTS

Portals are a fairly new concept. Portals are a personalised extension of the intranet concept, and just as many different types of information and activities went into intranets, so it will be with portals. Portals can be launched at the enterprise level and the HR components are able to provide an information or transactional feed; for example, a self-service or workflow application.

Component technology did not emerge overnight. It is the end result of Object-oriented Technology, which has been around for 20 years or more, maturing into a mainstream business technology solution. The underpinning concepts and design of CBT are related to object construction. The only difference between objects and components are size, referred to as degrees of granularity, and the way they are packaged. Components are packaged for commercial distribution, whereas objects are still very much the fine-grained building blocks of components.

From an HR business perspective, component based technology is exactly what is needed to support the fast moving, dynamic nature of the business. Current HRIS systems are seen as similar to an ocean going liner that takes too long to be turned around and headed in the new direction. Technology has to be far more nimble and adaptive to keep up with the changes to the HR business, changes brought about by new people in the HR Department, new ideas by the same people or change of mind (which is not altogether uncommon in HR).

The fact is, whether acknowledged or not by HR, most programs are doomed without technology support. Most new programs are driven by enthusiasm and hype rather than well planned projects supported by a solid HRIS infrastructure.

Concerning the professional facade enabled by CBT, the HR professionals who I see as one of the first adopters of and main beneficiaries of CBT applications, are the functional specialists. That is, the Human Resource Development Managers, or Training Managers or Recruitment Managers. They are desperately trying to sell a new HR program or concept and lack the technology tools to actually make it happen. The fact is, whether acknowledged or not by HR, most programs are doomed without technology support. Most new programs are driven by enthusiasm and hype rather than well planned projects supported by a solid HRIS infrastructure.

The CBT era will see the HR professional become more familiar with the capabilities of technology, and more aligned to a product that supports their preferred HR business program. There is a definite lack of originality in most HR programs and the technology requirements are all very similar. There is very little unique in a rewards program, compensation packaging, a "new" benefits program, a performance management program, a competency-based bonus scheme and so on. Consequently, most HRIS products are designed around a generic set of requirements. The differentiating factor in the future CBT era will focus on improving the business process. The continuous improvement process will be based on a synchronized effort between software capability and innovative business practice. At present, the inhibiting factor to continuous HR practice improvement is the software that an organization operates to launch the new program. It may mean major modifications to the current HRIS to capture the required information or to provide a feed back mechanism to managers. The business case to introduce the modifications must quantify something that is very difficult to assign a financial value to. This is often the case with HR type "products."

The component era will see HR professionals adopting a component software application as the right tool to assist the implementation of the program. Not only will the program gain credibility through capturing and reporting the right type of information, but it will overcome the current pitfall of trying to supplement existing HRIS with non-integrated standalone systems.

In the component era, the trend will come back to a form of in-house development, at the enterprise level, because software can be purchased as re-usable code in the form of objects.

In the CBT era, HR professionals will work more closely with developers to make sure that the component they wish to use has all the right features, to the point of providing detailed specifications so that the component can be tailored to their needs. The developer would obviously benefit by being able to on-sell the more business- aligned component application.

The HR professional will replace their little black diaries and hand-held computer gadgets with a more robustly networked PC with a personalized portal. The personalized portal would be connected to a component-based open and standards driven architecture, so that if they move to another organization they take their same PC and portal with them. The new organization simply plugs in the back end to the same component applications they are used to working with. If the new organization has a different component for performance appraisal or career development, then the choice is to unplug the old and plug in the new. The database layer is constant and does not change. Only the front-end does, in much the same way as you would expect your electrical appliances to plug into the new power system if you moved into a new house. You would not want to buy all new products and re-learn how to work the video, stereo and so on.

■ Examples of the change in thinking required for the CBT era

We are going to have to rethink some of our current beliefs about HR technology in the CBT era. For example, the following is the kind of statements that will require a change in thinking and decision-making:

"We should outsource the administrative functions and HR should only perform value-added functions."

CHANGE: The administrative functions are the very functions that technology has delivered productivity improvement benefits to in the last five years. The collection of forms-type information through workflow technology has greatly reduced the administrative effort in processing. The opposite should now apply. The functions that should be contracted in are the value-added functions. Short term assignments for HR program implementers (such as new benefits programs) should be referred to specialists consultancies. In that way, the latest and best business practices can be enjoyed by the organization. The end result is a more value-adding HR function and reduced administrative costs.

"Payroll does not add value so let us outsource."

CHANGE : The payroll operatives are most likely going to be the input source for a lot of HR type data in the line, such as new starter records, transfers and terminations. It is most unlikely that this function will be successful in the hands of anyone else. Also, most of the strategic HR information needed for decision making flows out of the payroll. There is a loss of flexibility and control over reporting. The problem of specific payroll product knowledge, making the payroll manager indispensable, or the fear of providing coverage for payroll people on leave, will go away with the CBT era. Payroll components will become far more standardized and many of the idiosyncrasies associated with older payroll products resulting from constraints that applied during the design stages of the systems, which made learning the product more difficult and payroll people more indispensable, will not apply.

"Let's outsource the whole thing to an application service provider (ASP) and avoid technology problems."

CHANGE: The ASP is no more likely to have the right software solution than you are. They would be using a proprietary system to run your business with sometimes less functionality than you now have. They try and make the software as generic as possible.

"Let's buy off-the-shelf packaged software; it is cheaper and easier."

CHANGE: In the component era, the trend will come back to a form of in-house development, at the enterprise level, because software can be purchased as re-usable code in the form of objects. The assembly of large systems, using integration specialists, will be less expensive, more flexible and provide a better functional fit. Like industries, such as universities can share code and software like never before.

"We should not purchase HR software before we perform a major business analysis and process review in order to select the best software fit."

CHANGE: In most cases, the review prior to purchase only ever picks up 60% of what is really required. The products rarely match more than 80% of those requirements. During implementation, the other 40% of the missed requirement becomes evident and that is when customization blows out the project cost. Much of the requirement from users relate to information retrieval and customized reports — not a standard feature of most HRIS products — which rely on ad hoc report writing tools for the user to build their own reports. Reports used in the old system can no longer run with the new product. Reports are components and can be plugged in the same as transactional applications. The process review is not necessary. Ownership of the process resides with the HR practitioner and they are the best ones to select the most appropriate component solution. They should be familiar with the products on the market. If they are not, then they are neglecting a major part of their role.

What is needed is something that delivers the right tools to the professional and the financial opportunity to developers to engage in competition to get the right products to the marketplace.

"The IT or HRIS group is the best group to select the new HR software."

CHANGE: The best people to select the new HR component are those performing the process. The selection of a new system should no longer follow the "big bang" approach. Aligning technology to process is an ongoing thing. In the component era, once the database and framework have been installed, the components are purchased and plugged in when needed. The same applies to replacement. If the process changes and a different component is more appropriate, then the old component is unplugged and replaced.

"I can customize my corporate system to meet overseas requirements."

CHANGE: An area that has failed to be addressed by the current generation of HR software is the trend towards globalization, and the large amount of localization that needs to be done to North American products to meet other country requirements. Componentization is the fastest way to solve the problem. If a Payroll component is required for Indonesia, then plug one in. If a Dormitory Administration component is required for China, then plug one in.

■ Visualizing the Future in a CBT Era

Let us visualize how things will look in the CBT era, starting with the organization. Every HR person, or person performing a people management role, or even a person wishing to view or change their own personal information, will interface to the "systems" through their own private portal. The knowledge sources that they have identified to do their job and keep up-to-date have been bookmarked and are accessible through the corporate network gateway to the Internet. Functional experts come with their own software solutions and provide the implementation support, such as training in the software and the business function. The HR department is a smaller outfit. The head of HR brings in specialists when required and keeps up-to-date on the latest trends in the industry. Administrative functions are linked to productivity tools such as self-service, workflow, interactive voice response (IVR) and so on.

Information technology departments have an internal resource of application integrators. HR is not the only component-based system and the enterprise architecture is such that HR components are stored in a corporate repository and accessed by more than one "system."

Every day, a new HR component comes onto the market supported by a new HR program or initiative. There is a progressive improvement in the overall quality of the HR function because it is delivered with the supporting technology. Practitioners are more aware of best practice in the industry and knowledge about improved processes and innovative practices is shared.

The potential of CBT is that it can reduce the overall cost of HRIS ownership by as much as 80%, when implementation and license costs are taken into consideration. The savings on replacement costs of HRIS, including new report libraries, etc., could be as high as 90%. By the end of the next decade, all HR systems will most likely be component-based.

If we were to base our assumptions on a philanthropic belief that people wanted the HR business unit to succeed regardless of what is happening to their personal careers, then that is not a solid base. Similarly, if we believe that HRIS vendors are about to provide the kind of systems that the HR professional needs by redesigning their current systems from the ground up, then that also will not happen. What is needed is something that delivers the right tools to the professional and the financial opportunity to developers to engage in competition to get the right products to the marketplace. Very early in the next decade there will be Component Markets and HR Application Standards. The Standards will not be driven by a body saying you must conform, but rather by the market pressures that will dictate that if a component product does not conform to the Standard then it wont be able to be sold. So, personal financial gain must play a major role in bringing about the shift in the way technology is currently developed.

John Macy is the Principal HR Consultant and Managing Director of Competitive Edge Technology, an Australian-based consulting business specialising in HRIS and he serves as an International Correspondent for the IHRIM Journal. He can be reached at **CET7@Compuserve.com**.

■ References

Graham, Henson-Sellers, and Younessi. *The OPEN process Specification* (ACM Press, New York / Addison-Wesley Longman Ltd, England, 1997. ISBN 0-201-331333-0)

Alex Berson. *Client/Server Architecture*, Second Edition (McGraw-Hill Series on Computer Communications, 1996. ISBN 0-07-005664-1)

Clemens Szyperski. *Component Software, Beyond Object-Oriented Programming* (ACM Press, New York / Addison-Wesley Longman Ltd, England, 1998. ISBN 0-201-17888-5)

Paul Allen and Stuart Frost. *Component-Based Development for Enterprise Systems, Applying the SELECT Perspective* (Course technology, Cambridge, MA 1998. ISBN 0-521-64999-4)

David A. Taylor. *Object Technology, A Manager's Guide* (Addison Wesley, 1997. ISBN 0-201-30994-7)

Reaz Hoque and Tarun Sharma. *WEB Components* (McGraw-Hill, 1998. ISBN 0-07-912316-3)

Desmond F. D'Souza and Alan Cameron Wills. *Objects, Components, and Frameworks with UML, The Catalysis Approach* (Addison Wesley, 1999. ISBN 0-201-31012-0)

Scott W. Ambler. *Building Object Applications That Work* (Cambridge University Press, 1998 ISBN. 0-521-64826-2)

Roger Fournier. *A Methodology for Client/Server and Web Application Development* (Prentice Hall, 1999. ISBN 0-13-598426-2)

Wayne C. Lim. *Managing Software Reuse, A Comprehensive Guide to Strategically Reengineering the Organization for Reusable Components* (Prentice Hall, 1998. ISBN 0-13-552373-7)

Mary Kirtland. *Designing Component-based Applications* (Microsoft Press, 1999. ISBN 0-7356-0523-8)

21st Century HRIS — The Network is the Employee

■ *The Knowledge Matrix*

As the economy moves from refining existing products and services for mass audiences to innovating and personalizing new products and services, the knowledge used, and how it is used, changes. Business knowledge can be sorted into one of the four quadrants of the Knowledge Matrix[1] below. Complexity and uncertainty increase as we move from the first quadrant (Q1) to the last quadrant (Q4).

Q1 is easy — it is what we know that we know. We can easily access this knowledge within ourselves or our groups and share it with others. Q2 is almost as straightforward. Q2 contains what we are aware of that we do not know. Some of what we do not know we may wish to learn through education, training or apprenticeship and job experience. Others things we may wish to leave in the "don't know" pile. Q3 becomes a little tricky. In individuals, it is things we know but are not totally aware that we know. These are either hidden skills or

Figure 1.

Q1: We know what we know	Q2: We know what we don't know
Q3: We don't know what we know	Q4: We don't know what we don't know

133

knowledge you have temporarily forgotten. In groups, this is knowledge and skills that part of the group has but another part of the group does not — nor is this other part of the group aware that this knowledge and skill exists elsewhere in the group. Subgroup A knows; Subgroup B does not know; nor does B know that A knows. Q4 is the blind spot for individuals and groups. We can't answer the question "What is in Q4 for you?" We don't know! Q4 is almost always involved with businesses that fail to adapt to changes in their environment. This is from where unseen and unknown competition arises.

■ 20th Century Knowledge Processing

It is obvious that knowledge will drive the value chains of businesses in the future. In many ways, knowledge was a competitive advantage in the old industrial economy also. All inventions from the steam engine to the light bulb were the result of knowledge processes. Henry Ford's assembly line was the result of a knowledge process that provided the Ford organization a competitive advantage for many years. The focus was on the select individual — the solitary genius — the lone ranger. Inputs and learning from the group were not rewarded. In fact, participant's on the assembly line were actively encouraged to leave their brains at home. The manager knew what was right — no one else need contribute feedback. In the industrial era our focus in the knowledge matrix was on Quadrants 1 and 2.

Executives and managers started to sense the existence of Quadrant 4. "Why didn't we see it coming?" was the common conundrum in boardrooms as we entered the new millennium.

In the information economy of 1970-2000, knowledge processes where pushed out from genius inventors to a growing population of college educated knowledge workers. Rather than toiling without thinking on assembly lines like their parents, a new generation was asked to bring their brains to work and use them. Unfortunately, there was no Henry Ford who could build an assembly line of knowledge work — though some tried. It soon became obvious that many similar projects were all being done without utilizing what had been learned on previous projects. The wheel was constantly being reinvented. The smart thinkers of the later part of the 20th century noticed that learning and knowledge were not shared — many of us don't know what others already know. Quadrant 3 in the matrix was revealed. Soon, knowledge management (KM) was born to capture and store "what we know" and make it available to those that need to know. Unfortunately, applying Henry Ford style thinking, which many short-sighted KM efforts tried, did not work with knowledge processes that demanded adaption, learning and innovation.

The Internet economy started quickly in the mid 1990s and was in full steam at the turn of the century. Many smart, profitable companies were slow to adapt to the changes of this new connectivity amongst business players. Many of these companies were blind-sided by new competitors "coming out of nowhere." Players like Amazon and Wal Mart created whole new ways of doing business using the power of information and network connectivity. Executives and managers started to sense the existence of Quadrant 4. "Why didn't we see it coming?" was the common conundrum in boardrooms as we entered the new millennium.

Some companies stumbled onto Q4 and profited from their serendipitous discovery. Thanks to a few vocal and persistent employees with the ear of key executives, one company — Microsoft, learned very quickly what it didn't know it didn't know. As a result of this "aha,"the whole mission of the organization was refocused on the Internet. The ability to access Q4 probably saved Microsoft and their market-leading position. All of the formal strategic planning and business intelligence processes failed to illuminate what was happening in Q4. These formal processes were most likely focused on Q2, with some attention to Q3. It was serendipity and the informal networks that exposed what was happening in Q4 to Bill Gates and other key decision-makers within Microsoft. Once Q4 was discovered the knowledge moved into Q2, and Microsoft could focus on learning everything it could about Internet technology and dynamics.

By the turn of the millennium all successful organizations were expert at developing knowledge in Q1 and Q2. Many where working out the kinks in Q3 and only the cutting edge firms were even aware of Q4.

■ The Network is the Employee

In the 21st century, we have to keep our gains in Q1 and Q2 knowledge processing, improve our ability for including Q3 knowledge, and develop new skills and methods for discovering and mining Q4 knowledge. Both Q3 and Q4 knowledge processing will be improved with the power of the network.

Everyone will be on the interconnected Web. Internal webs will be present in each company, while business partners will have connections between their respective internal webs. The trick for finding Q3 knowledge will be the ability to surf the network and know what each sub-web contains. Parts of the web will know what knowledge and experience is available in other parts of the web. Projects will be composed of many sub-webs usually spanning the formal borders of individual organizations.

The ability to quickly assemble and disassemble many component webs into a larger networked whole will be the competitive advantage one project team as over others. Connected teams will compete with connected teams. Agility of connecting, disconnecting, and reconnecting will be one focus of competitive advantage. The other hub of advantage will be utilizing the pattern of connections you have formed. Can information quickly traverse your network? Is you network aware of what is happening outside the network? Does the pattern of connections have the right mix of redundancy for learning and agility— not too much and not too little?

The ability to quickly assemble and disassemble many component webs into a larger networked whole will be the competitive advantage one project team has over others. Connected teams will compete with connected teams.

Q3 knowledge will be accessed and utilized by the right pattern of connections between sub-webs in the larger group. Q4 knowledge will be discovered and transferred by links from the various sub-webs out to the environment. Close, redundant ties implement group goals. Radial, non-redundant ties monitor the environment and discover threats or opportunities for the group.

■ *HRIS of the Future*

The HRIS of the future will differ from the HRIS of today like the road network of the 20th century differed from the roads in Ancient Rome. All roads lead to Rome — there was one central point of focus. A central repository of employee data supported the business processes of recruiting, retention, payroll, and benefits. The processes of producing revenue such as product development and fulfillment rarely if ever utilized the HRIS — they had their own Rome — another central repository of data. Toward the end of the 20th century, new systems came into fashion that attempted to connect these independent resources. They succeeded in connecting everything, but did so in a rigid way — they were not easily adaptable to rapidly changing business processes. The speed of change brought on by the Internet soon led to cracks in, and then crumbling of, these rigid, engineered structures. At the turn of the millennium, many companies which had installed systems that automated business processes started to experience problems in delivering products and services to their customers. Many a well-known company made announcement after announcement that their quarterly results would not meet expectations because of their inability to deliver the right mix of products in the right quantity to the right customers. It was 2001 and HAL was indeed alive — no more science fiction. He was alive and in control of the ship. Many a CEO, COO, CFO and CIO died trying to negotiate with the wayward, all-controlling computer.

The HRIS of the future will not be a "system" — it will be a navigator of, and a tool for, building temporary knowledge structures. It will not be focused solely on traditional HR business processes. It will be a key tool in accomplishing the day-to-day work within and between organizations. The aim will not be to build large stores of data and information recorded in silicon. The HRIS of the future will be a network of human and silicon nodes. The key will not be efficient storage of data items, but efficient paths to the knowledge and data necessary to accomplish current projects. The HRIS of the future will be like the road system of today. When traveling you can choose any combinations of roads depending on your travel plans. The interstate highway for speed, the back roads for scenery, or something in between. The interstate from point A to B, two-lane highway from point B to C, and then the old scenic trails from C to D. The return trip may require a different combination.

The HRIS of the future will not be a "system" — it will be a navigator of, and a tool for, building temporary knowledge structures. It will not be focused solely on traditional HR business processes.

In the industrial economy, the key was individual objects organized in a hierarchy. Paths to negotiate the hierarchy were predetermined and followed strict rules. In the new economy, the connections between objects become as important, or more, than the objects themselves. The links, and the pattern of links, in the network are as important as the nodes. Paths are not predetermined. Rules for traveling the network are limited only by security access privileges. Power is no longer accrued by gathering the most or the largest objects under your hierarchy. Power is gained by being well-positioned in the network of information flows and knowledge exchanges. Those with access to the right parts of the network have access to all four quadrants in the Knowledge Matrix.

The key is connectivity — finding the right patterns of connections to produce the desired results for the current goals. As strategy and goals change, so do the patterns of connections, and so does network membership. Different combinations for different collaborations.

Valdis Krebs is an organizational consultant, author, and contributing columnist for the IHRIM Jour-nal. *He can be reached at* **valdis@orgnet.com**.

■ References

Figure 1. Knowledge Matrix based on work originally developed and copyrighted by Land-mark Education Corporation, San Francisco, California.

Tomorrow's HR Systems:
Technologies
With a Human Face

By Robert H. Stambaugh

For history buffs, the current millennialism isn't a new occurrence. It happened a thousand years ago, and there was the same sense of promise and the same expectations of deliverance from our problems then that we are experiencing now. A thousand years ago, people expected a religious deliverance; we're now awaiting a similar *deus ex machina* from technology. Will technology respond and eliminate current obstacles to satisfying the needs of Human Resources and its stakeholders? Should we forge ahead now or wait for the next quantum leap in software packages after CRM and ERP? And if we should wait, is there anything we can do in the meantime to improve the lot of HRIS stakeholders on a day-to-day basis?

For HRIS in the decade to come, enticing new clients and keeping old ones will mean knowing the business and the clientele well enough to create, package, and deliver information and knowledge products that are reinvented every day.

I think the answers to these questions are largely subjective and can be discerned from what we believe about four key areas. Who will our clients be in the coming decade? What will they ask us to do for them? What will need to be done that they can't see now? And, how can we employ our expertise and understanding about technology in a way that most benefits them?

Let's address these questions one at a time.

■ The HRIS Marketplace: Clients, Prospects and Targets of Opportunity

As outsourcing expands, external sources will quickly claim as their own territory most of the day-to-day repetitive activities we address with internal systems today. They'll penetrate our internal markets because processes and functions that can be defined and modeled will become commodities. It will become cheaper and more efficient to spin off administration and "business-as-usual" to these outsiders, whose practices, by the way, will almost certainly be certified as "standard" by some industry-wide body. This trend would take on mammoth proportions if the make-up of the workforce were to remain similar to today's workforce composition, but an accompanying trend of shrinkage among full-time, "permanent" staff will continue, and perhaps accelerate, as the decade unfolds. HR and HRIS will be left with a significantly smaller employee core population and much reduced service demands.

In yesterday's workplace, HRIS support would have required much greater specialization within the corporate HR function; in the emerging workplace, it means access to a network of advisors who collaborate across a dozen or more disciplines to determine costs and value.

A good thing, too, since decreases in numbers will not result in a decrease in total need. That's because almost every core employee will be treated as a special case, from the time of first pre-recruitment contact, all the way through his or her career and on to initial separation. Depending upon one's point of view, the need to develop special packages to attract and retain key talent will change HR dramatically: HR representatives will be both talent scouts and agents (the employees' view!) or producers and impresarios for a succession of company-funded projects (the corporate perspective). Since core staff will be scarce and valuable commodities, HR's visibility and potential clout in the workplace will skyrocket, if it can insure a supply of top-quality employees and affiliates.

In their role as talent scouts, we'll watch HR scour the channels that feed corporate recruiting for potential future performers. I believe we'll see Human Resources develop semi-formal and long-term relationships that go far beyond traditional sourcing, linking to groups ranging from cartels of contractor/consultants to individual high schools, employment agencies and professional societies. Where analyses of performance and long-term retention identify "star" suppliers, HR will be administering programs that include funding, summer employment, and even distance training beginning as early as junior high school years.

At the other end of the spectrum, HR will also be working with "first-time" retirees to secure their part-time presence in a network of back-up associates, perhaps arranging for small retainers to assure availability, and almost certainly coordinating distance learning to keep these potential workers up to date with their competencies and corporate cultures.

Today's HR and HRIS infrastructure will disappear. Standard report libraries, corporate data definitions, and the like will become a joint responsibility of IT production groups and their outsourcing partners. HR's external contacts, corporate clients, individual employees, and small groups or communities of practice will all demand something different — total, unabridged product personalization. None of them will bother to use standard HR systems unless they too become highly individualized.

For HRIS in the decade to come, enticing new clients and keeping old ones will mean knowing the business and the clientele well enough to create, package, and deliver information and knowledge products that are reinvented every day. Our role will shift from product developer to service provider. It will also require developing and maintaining broad and comprehensive networks that keep individuals in contact and reinforce common divisional or corporate-wide values and goals. "Contact" will occur mainly through informal networks; "reinforcement" will take place via approved corporate channels.

■ What Will Tomorrow's Markets Demand?

Knowledge of all kinds — HR, Administrative, Organizational, and Technology-related — is growing explosively as we leave the 20th century, and there is every reason to expect that trend to continue — and accelerate. Individuals in HR and its client communities will no longer be able to absorb, let alone master, the range of skills and competencies that we have come to expect in the current workplace. They will have to choose narrower and narrower specialty areas, while allying themselves with a group of other specialists in the company and outside its boundaries. These virtual teams will together deliver the same breadth of information as individuals a decade earlier, but in greater depth and less expense.

This need to be in contact with "state of the art" will become a critical success factor in tomorrow's workplace, and Human Resources will be expected to define its structure, apply it to every one of the enterprises microclimates, support it administratively, and if we choose — lead it toward a strategic perspective. The implications for HRIS are fourfold.

First, clients will want us to locate and coordinate true sources of information and knowledge for the enterprise at large, wherever such nuggets exist, and then develop on-the-spot compensation/rewards that allow our bidding for the necessary services in an open labor market. No more compa-ratios. No more salary bands, broadbanding, range penetration analysis, or quintile reports. Salary planning and compensation administration will become real-time, five-minute exercises that we pursue relentlessly. The only determinant of a current or prospective employee's worth will be what he or she can command in 24x7 auctions over the Internet — and HRIS needs to participate throughout the entire process. We will become the service that HR uses for demands such as these.

...HRIS vendors, consultants, and practitioners alike will finally learn to talk to each other as partners in the same market space, and they will jointly and constantly comb a variety of related disciplines to uncover tools and techniques that can be applied to the workplace.

Second, and beyond the simple service/support roles just described, clients will want increasingly sophisticated measurement of employee worth. Such calculations will be one part salary-related, with another part based upon benefits and cost of training. In addition, they will include highly subjective (and when well conceived and modeled, unbelievably valuable) proprietary algorithms that project individual and team current and future potential for strategic projects. These capabilities will be expressed in financial terms, but also in powerful graphic simulations and 3-D analyses. In yesterday's workplace, HRIS support would have required much greater specialization within the corporate HR function; in the emerging workplace, it means access to a network of advisors who collaborate across a dozen or more disciplines to determine costs and value.

Third, we will be asked to monitor constantly employee and contingent players — their ebbs and flows, the groups they join, and the capabilities they offer as individuals, teams, and communities. When we discover actual or projected shortages or a looming absence of capabilities, we will be expected to direct repair of the impacted communities and clients without adverse business impacts, and without excessive involvement of local operations staff. HRIS "power" will be the source of capabilities for analyses and action that constantly shapes, not just the enterprise's workforce, but the entire network of potential workers and competencies at home and in cyberspace.

This new role implies developing (or linking to) corporate anthropologists and communications specialists, sociologists and organizational development personnel. We'll need to build and develop online communities whose look and feel attracts and then helps retain key talent, since the draw of other such communities will be only one or two URL's away.

We have a choice as to whether we want to approach this challenge mechanically — by concentrating on the pure technology of networks and ourselves becoming experts, or of hiring the network specialists and shifting our roles to design and planning.

We don't have a choice about the technology vehicle we'll be using: again, it's internal and external networks.

■ What Should We Be Planning for The Day After Tomorrow?

If there's one general business lesson we can learn from the innovators in Silicon Valley, it's that today's successes are tomorrow's vulnerabilities. We need to be planning for the creation of new and innovative products and services now, long before there is a widely perceived demand for them, and then we need to publicize and "sell" our new offerings at home and outside the corporation before someone else comes up with the same idea and takes our markets away from us. We will draw and retain talent by being ahead of the technology curve, and by being perceived as offering the best and most leading-edge place to work. This kind of thinking may sound awfully entrepreneurial to someone listening with a 1999 viewpoint, but it will be a very mainstream concept by 2005.

With this challenge on the horizon, I think HRIS vendors, consultants, and practitioners alike will finally learn to talk to each other as partners in the same market space, and they will jointly and constantly comb a variety of related disciplines to uncover tools and techniques that can be applied to the workplace. We'll see more and more market research tools (data mining and analysis "cubes," for example) in our portfolio — we'll analyze, stratify, and target our individual clients and stakeholders. We will continually create and package mini-data bases, reports, and queries that may appeal to them, based on their recent past and present information usage behavior profiles. That will require us to monitor individual and group information usage, and we'll be as quick to discard slow-moving products as would be any supermarket or discount store.

There's another reason for this monitoring behavior: we'll be part of a tidal wave of new and improved package-based information and reporting, the cumulative effect of which will leave our customers overwhelmed, dazed, and suffering from an almost terminal case of information overload. Our challenge will be to scour everything from videogames to weekly e-magazines to find formats and "shticks" to facilitate delivery and discussion, and that grab customer attention. While this phenomenon may start slowly in 2001 and 2002, it will mushroom as "Nintendo generation" managers begin to appear in the workforce later in the decade.

And we'll be distributing these new reports and tools on a daily basis, for trials or beta tests, as shareware or loss leaders for more advanced, more consultative HR systems services. After all, we will be the people who know and understand key information in employee and contractor databases. By the way, the distribution will be — you guessed it — almost entirely an Internet event. And we'll be offering it as a service, relying on others to develop a commodity level package.

■ *Technology — In Beneficial Doses*

At the risk of sounding a little "techno phobic," I think the really critical new role for HRIS professionals and managers will revolve around protecting Human Resource staff and the enterprise's "crown jewels" core workforce from largely unintended impacts of galloping technology.

I've already mentioned the phenomenon of information overload or data smog. HRIS needs to identify and eliminate the worst offenders in this area, most of whom will be third-party providers who do not understand the difference between information and knowledge in the products and reports they deliver. We'll need to offer "top 10" and "bottom 10" lists of added-value information sources.

I think we'll also have to weigh and balance the legitimate and quasi-legitimate demands of the enterprise for more information about its actual and potential/virtual workforce against employee concerns for information ownership and privacy. There are solid arguments from both camps, and HR/HRIS may find itself as the sole impartial go-between in the emerging interconnected corporate environment. If our systems remain worldwide in scope and reach, we'll also be challenged by different cultural views of information "appropriate" for sharing and use in the business community. For an industry that has been largely influenced by American and Western European values and practices, it will be a major challenge to set aside what have become self-righteous and almost arrogant positions about individual privacy, in a world where many cultures have different values.

We'll have to advise our companies when to "invest" in new systems, and we have to insist that they enter into new systems initiatives with eyes wide open, understanding not just yesterday's return on investment (ROI) concepts, but the risks and operating principles of e-commerce and how it applies in the HR environment. We'll likewise need to be critical observers of performance by current outsourcing partnerships, and we'll need the courage to call for changes when performance so indicates.

I don't believe we can do these things by ourselves: technology and disciplines that are "neighbors" to our HR communities are all changing too fast for us to keep up. It will take trusting and long-term alliances with one or more consulting firms or system houses to assure access to the breadth of knowledge we need when we advise our client base — that's a major explanation for the emphasis on knowledge management we see today among the major consultancies. It will also take links to other firms in our industries, geographical areas, business lines — sometimes even with competitors to build new technology "early warning systems" that make sense of tomorrow's products and services before they reach our doorsteps.

... the new generation of HR workers, IT, and their outsourcing partners can now handle the basics with only an occasional need for our help.

And, all these links will rely on the Internet and its connections to the corporate world through a web of internal networks.

■ Summary: Opportunities — and Obligations

As a discipline, HRIS has spent the last 30 years supporting technology products. That practice goes back to a time when data processing was so new and so removed from the day-to-day experience of HR that we had no other choice when we developed our business style. As we enter the new millennium, we need to recognize that our infancy is behind us; the new generation of HR workers, IT, and their outsourcing partners can now handle the basics with only an occasional need for our help.

What we need to do is apply the experience we have gained in three decades or more to the emerging world of networks, networking and service delivery — so that our stakeholders see the same level of operational excellence from HR systems that they experience when they access commercial service providers from their easy chairs at home.

Succeed at this, and we'll be regarded as a strategic asset everywhere in the organization. Fail, and by 2010 we'll be just another outsourced service provider, with about as much impact on a business as the services we hire today to water the flowers.

Bob Stambaugh is President of Kapa'a Associates, a Hawaii-based consulting firm specializing in using information technology to improve organizational effectiveness. He is a member of the IHRIM Board of Directors and the Editorial Advisory Board of the IHRIM Journal. He can be reached at **stambaugh-kapaa@worldnet.att.net**.

Organisations
and HR
in the 2000s

By Juan Vila

■ *Change, change, change*

Everytime we reach the end of the year, and even more, the end of a decade, we have the habit of making an assessment of the most relevant things that have happened during the period. At this time, we always feel that things have changed faster than ever before. We are overwhelmed by the speed and magnitude of the changes that have taken place.

I believe this feeling is particularly significant in the 1990s. If we take a quick look at the decade that has just ended, practically all of us will agree that there has not been any other decade in which so many changes have been experienced by humankind and which have had such important effects on our everyday life. The 90s will go down into history, or at least in our own personal history, as years in which the world changed radically. Life after the 90s will never be the way it was before. From a social economic standpoint, the world geography changed during the last decade. Europe is a good example, with the unification of Germany and the new nations which have sprouted up since the breakup of the Soviet Union, an economic system (the communist), which was followed by a substantial part of the world collapsed after 70 years and a new currency — the euro — used by a whole continent was born and, new economies began to emerge in underdeveloped countries just a few years ago. And, what about technology? In a very short number of years, the mobile telephone has spread in such a way that it has changed our habits and those of our children. Something that may have seemed like science fiction back in the

1980s (making a phone call from anywhere you want using a device that is the same size as a credit card) can be bought for a few dollars at any department store. PCs, laptops, and graphic interfaces have all made information technology a core part of our everyday life and work.

In the 90s, technology created a new landscape in our organisations, which have been subjected to a continual redefinition processes. Things as simple as e-mail and intranets, let alone the plethora of business applications, brought about thorough changes in business processes.

And, of course, the Internet. A phenomenon with effects as yet not understood. Something, which just a few years back was reserved to university students, researchers and techies, has become one of the driving forces of the world economy and society in general.

■ So, if this is what happened in the last 10 years, what will happen in the next 10 years?

If, at the beginning of the 90s, someone with a crystal ball had shown us everything that would happen over the next 10 years, we would have looked at the soothsayer incredulously. Reality, however, has surpassed the most prolific imagination. Could something similar happen in the decade that is now starting? In my opinion the decade beginning in the year 2000 will bring about many more changes than the crazy 90s. If, in the past decade, we had the feeling that our world was changing radically, it will be nothing compared to what the new decade has in store.

On what is such a radical view based? On the growth rate of technological developments. It is my opinion, that the speed of change increases as technology — particularly communication technology — develops. And, as I see it, the communication revolution has only just begun. In the late 90s, we saw the Internet take off and the explosion of cellular phone technology. Today, we are witnessing the early stages of WAP technology (cellular access to the Internet). If Moore's Law is accurate, the power of microprocessors will continue to increase two-fold every 18 months and their price will decline by half in the same period. Bandwidth will grow dramatically, with spectacular cost reductions, and as a result we shall soon have ubiquitous Internet connection facilities, with virtually unimaginable processing power at anyone's fingertips. Our entire life (not only our work, of course) will be connected: mobile phones, cars, domestic appliances, etc. And, all these changes will develop at an exponential rate.

■ Change of paradigm, change of the organisational ecosystem

The past decade brought about the onset of a change of paradigm which will become fully apparent beginning in the year 2000. The industrial age is giving way to the information age. The focus of value is moving from tangible to intangible goods. In fact, today the most highly valued companies in the stock market are those with the least material possessions. The greater part of value, as suggested by Leif Edvinson, lies in the Intellectual Capital of Organisations. The focus on productivity improvements, which was widespread in the industrial age, is being replaced by the focus on innovation, which is a key factor of the knowledge society.

The capacity of an organisation and its individuals to effectively react to the ongoing changes taking place at all levels — technology, society, culture, politics, economics — will be key in the coming years.

At the end of the day, the new paradigm is creating a new landscape, new living conditions, at such a fast pace that organisations will have to learn to adapt themselves very quickly if they do not want to be doomed to evanescence. It looks like the new paradigm, led by the technological revolution, will create new forms of business life after the year 2000, new business models as yet unknown, which will emerge and grow in the new virtual society. I am almost certain that the current business models, the organisational model as we see it today, will have little in common with what will be in place at the end of this decade. We can already see how the Internet is giving rise to countless companies, with ever sophisticated business models that are far removed from tradition. And, this is only the beginning, given the limitations in terms of speed and access to the Internet. What will happen when bandwidth becomes unlimited and ubiquitous?

■ And, what will we have to do from an HR standpoint?

If it is true that the decade beginning in the year 2000 will be an unprecedented period of change, it seems daring to even hint at what the HR role might be because reality is likely to surprise us no matter what assumptions we make.

So, instead of trying to be soothsayers, let's analyse a number of permanent circumstances that, as I perceive it, will prevail no matter what the final landscape turns out to be:

1. *Adaptability* — in an environment of increasing, ongoing change, the most highly prized value will be adaptability — the ability to continually adapt to changing conditions. What Darwin taught us about species still fully applies to organisations and the business world. The capacity of an organisation and its individuals to effectively react to the ongoing changes taking place at all levels — technology, society, culture, politics, economics — will be key in the coming years.

... one of the core roles of the HR function will be to prepare the organisation so that every manager and every employee is capable of managing their own personal and career potential development, as well as that of their collaborators.

2. *Network organisation* — it is increasingly harder to define where an organisation begins and where it ends. Until recently, an organisation was something inside an office building or a factory. As complexity increases, an organisation needs to spread out and become a network in which each part of the organisation is able to react to change locally, to learn how to efficiently respond to and interact with other elements, and with other similar organisations to which it is related. As a result, an organisation becomes a conglomerate of individuals — working within the organisation, and with external collaborators, distributors, suppliers, clients — all of whom are linked by common objectives.

In such a landscape, it looks like the most important thing in an organisation is how its intellectual capital is managed. The focus will be on its intangible assets: managing individuals, managing their knowledge, aligning the organisation as a network working towards common goals, and sharing common values. This may undoubtedly lead to a repositioning of the HR function at the core of organisational management. Based on these assumptions, what could the mission of HR be in the coming decade?

From a very general standpoint, it seems like its main mission will be to help the organisation so that it is permanently in a situation of efficient adaptation. Now, of course, this objective will not be left to HR exclusively, because for each and every one of the members of the organisation, managing intellectual capital will be a key focal point. And, precisely one of the core roles of the HR function will be to prepare the organisation so that every manager and every employee is capable of managing their own personal and career potential development, as well as that of their collaborators.

We have seen how organisations become networks in order to efficiently manage the complexity and environment of change. A thorough understanding of the behaviour of a network entails understanding what HR will have to do in the coming decade.

In a network, each part needs an extraordinary degree of autonomy to learn from the environment and react accordingly. But, at the same time, an organisation cannot be an anarchistic network. It needs to produce. It needs to show the world and market a homogeneous and stable appearance. Now, as I see it, this will be the critical mission of HR function — helping the organisation become a network while pursuing common objectives. This will probably configure some critical HR tasks:

... new life forms will appear in an increasingly virtual world. HR will have to learn to manage — through the network — the same asset that has always been the key factor in organisations — its people.

1. *Managing common values* — a sense of identity shared by all the members of the network, including the "extended company." In other words, not only those in the organisation's payroll, but also those individuals helping to achieve the company's goals by sharing a common intellectual capital.

2. *Managing the knowledge and learning of the organisation as a whole* — in this respect, it is essential to prepare the organisation so that it includes the management of knowledge among its cultural values. HR must create the environment for the continual creation and sharing of knowledge — an environment in which those who create and share enjoy proper recognition.

3. *Developing remuneration systems* — which favour networking, incorporating not only variables related to the company's income or its stock market performance, but also other variables related to aspects such as innovation, creation and sharing of knowledge.

4. *Having a thorough understanding of the opportunities that become available thanks to technology* — the future of HR seems to be increasingly linked to the future of technology. Of course, this does not mean that HR professionals are to become chief technology officers (CTOs), but they must understand the profound impact that technology can have on managing the organisation. Whether an organisation works like a network will rely heavily on how it uses technology. There will be many opportunities to make the most of technology in order to manage knowledge, to organise "just-in-time" (JIT) training systems across the network, to create knowledge-sharing networks among the members of the "extended company," and to create communities of trust across the network. HR

will have to create new management approaches in companies where relations with employees will increasingly take place through networks. As I mentioned at the beginning, new life forms will appear in an increasingly virtual world. HR will have to learn to manage — through the network — the same asset that has always been the key factor in organisations — its people.

■ Summary

If we are surprised by the huge changes which have taken place in the 90s (the breakup of the Soviet Union, the demise of the communist economic model, the appearance of cellular telephony, the Internet explosion), surely what happens in the next decade will be even more surprising. Unimagined today, technology will create such forms of business life and work which will surely change the current business models we are familiar with in a radical way.

Because of this, the only certainty we have today regarding the decade beginning in the year 2000 is that change will be overwhelming. And, we are sure that the most prized value in the next decade will be adaptability. All management efforts should work in this direction, thus the consistent tendency of organisations to become networks is a response to the need of permanently adapting.

The mission of the Human Resources department should be to help the organisation work like an intelligent network: its parts will be fully autonomous, but they will all work towards the attainment of a common goal. Because of this, working on values and culture, on managing knowledge, on imaginative remuneration schemes, and always taking stock of technology and making the most of it, will be key factors for the HR function in the decade beginning in the year 2000.

---

*Juan Vila is the Vice Chairman of the Board of Meta4. Founded in Madrid in 1991, Meta4 develops and implements its software products and is also a solution partner for Baan. He serves on the Editorial Advisory Board of the IHRIM Journal and can be reached at **juanv@meta4.es**.*

■ References

Peter Drucker, "The Age of Social Transformation," *Atlantic Monthly*, November 1994.

Leif Edvinson and Michael S. Malone, *Intellectual Capital*, 1997.

Juan Vila, "People and Knowledge: Two sides of the same coin." *IHRIM Journal*, September 1998.

International
Association for
Human Resource
Information Management

The mission of the International Association for Human Resource Information Management is to be the leading global source of knowledge for the application of human resource information and technology to improve organizational effectiveness.

IHRIM is the only organization of its kind. We exclusively serve the increasingly complex human resources information management profession. Through a full complement of dynamic educational programs, products, services and events, IHRIM has provided information, ideas and answers to HRIM, HRIS, HR and IT professionals for 20 years. This outstanding book is just one tangible example of our leadership and vision.

We invite you to learn more about us and how we can help you drive greater organizational effectiveness through strategic human resources information management.

Join us! For more information about IHRIM membership and IHRIM programs, visit **www.ihrim.org**, email **moreinfo@ihrim.org**, or call **+1.312.321.5141**.

Sincerely,

B. Lynn DeLeo
Chairman of the Board and President
International Association for Human
Resource Information Management